Civil War
Ghosts

By
Michelle Hamilton

Michelle Hamilton

First Edition:
First printing

Michelle Hamilton

PUBLISHED BY HAUNTED ROAD MEDIA, LLC
www.hauntedroadmedia.com

United States of America

This book is dedicated to the memory of my aunt Vickie Shubert and my dog Pearl who passed away this year.

Michelle Hamilton

Acknowledgments

I would like to thank the following individuals:

This project would not have been completed without the love and support of my parents. Mom and Dad, I love you.

I would like to thank Courtney Cutler for providing helpful edits to the introduction. It is a pleasure to work with you.

To my advisor and friend, Dr. Edward Blum, thank you for thinking that this project had merit.

Thank you, Mike Ricksecker and Haunted Road Media, for accepting my manuscript and for welcoming me into the Haunted Road Media family.

Michelle Hamilton

$\mathcal{T}able\ of\ \mathcal{C}ontents$

Michelle Hamilton

Introduction

America in the Civil War era (1860-1865) was a haunted country. The sins of slavery preyed upon the nation, and its chains had woven into virtually every facet of society, rendering deep divisions. By 1860, the debate over slavery could no longer be contained. The election of Abraham Lincoln as the sixteenth President of the United States brought simmering tensions to the surface and spilt the nation apart, resulting in a long and bloody civil war.

America was also haunted by ghosts during the Civil War. Americans were encountering the unknown and mysterious on street corners, in their parlors, at public places and even in military installations. The nation was obsessed with ghosts. This may come as a surprise to some modern readers who may consider the current fascination with ghosts and the paranormal as a recent invention. Popular shows such as *Ghost Hunters* and *Ghost Adventures* and the myriad other television shows and documentaries that flood television airways are only the current manifestations of a long national interest in the paranormal.

Even prior to the Civil War, Americans have loved a good ghost story. The early European immigrants that settled the original thirteen colonies were primarily from the United Kingdom (England, Scotland, Ireland and Wales) and Germany. These cultures already had a rich folklore and legends about ghosts and mysterious creatures that went bump in the night. The new world that these immigrants found was dark and obscure. Veiled woods teemed with strange wildlife. Hostile Native Americans lurked in the shadows. Leaving the confines of the home could be fatal. To cope with the unknown, early colonists transplanted their ghost stories and moved them to North America. On long, cold winter nights, ghost stories were recounted to while away the hours.

The high mortality rates during the Eighteenth and Nineteenth-Centuries were reflected in the focus on death and mourning. For Nineteenth-Century Americans, death could strike at any moment. A sudden chill could result in a fatal illness in a matter of hours. Death during this period occurred at home. The dying were surrounded by family and friends who carefully monitored every utterance made to ensure that a good death occurred. To have a good death, the person had to be aware of his or her fate—so pain killing medication was highly discouraged. The dying were also expected to pass on words of comfort to the living, preferably of a religious nature. Sudden death from accidents, warfare, murder, or suicide were viewed as a bad death and left their surviving loved ones with little comfort. It should be no surprise that these unfortunate deaths formed the heart of Nineteenth-Century ghost stories.

In 1848, the Fox family was disturbed from their slumber by mystifying knocking sounds. The family determined that a ghost was responsible and that the activity was at its strongest when sisters Kate and Maggie Fox were present. Neighbors flocked to the farmhouse located in Hydesville, New York, to witness the phenomena and were shocked that they could communicate with the ghost responsible for the activity. Soon, other ghosts in the neighborhood appeared and communication with them was established. Out of these humble beginnings, Spiritualism emerged as a religious movement that spread across the country in a matter of months. Spiritualist circles or séances were held in parlors across the nation, and contacting the dead became a parlor amusement.

Popular culture reflected Americans interest in the paranormal. Spirits of the dead flitted through the works of popular literature from the *Headless Horsemen* to the poems and stories of Edgar Allan Poe. While the works of Poe and Washington Irving were fictional, Catherine Crowe and Robert Dale Owen published books that recounted real life accounts of the paranormal. Newspapers responded to the demand, and columns were filled with accounts of ghosts wondering the streets of American towns and cities. Naturally, these reports created numerous hoaxes. A popular phenomenon of the time was for young men to dress up as a ghost to scare late night travelers.

The Civil War only fueled American interest in ghosts. The carnage of the war brought death to the forefront as soldiers were dying on the battlefields, hospitals, and prisons. Soldiers were dying away from their homes and families. Even as the war was going on, people were reporting seeing the ghosts of Civil War soldiers.

This book is a collection of the best ghost accounts published in American newspapers during the Civil War. The accounts range from the spine-tingling to the humorous. You will read about the ghosts of Civil War soldiers in hospitals and prisons, a ghost spotted in a New York City library, and a haunted church among other accounts. I hope these accounts give you a sense and appreciation of the paranormal culture of the Nineteenth Century and will advance your knowledge of this time period.

Michelle Hamilton

1860

Daily Dispatch, Richmond, Virginia
January 13, 1860, pg. 1.

A LOVE-SICK GHOST.—A servant girl, who had been for a long time with a highly respectable family on Morgan street, St. Louis, left the house of her mistress, recently, stating that for several nights she had been visited by a tall, fearful-looking spectre, dressed in a long white robe. She got up one night and tried to strike him, but he vanished out of sight. Once or twice the ghost was impudent enough to come and sit on the side of the poor girl's bed. Her mistress tried to persuade her that her fears were groundless, but she went away, declaring that she would not live in a house with ghosts.

New Orleans Daily Crescent, New Orleans, Louisiana, January 16, 1860, pg. 2

A Trip from Camp Floyd to Los Angeles.
FROM CAMP FLOYD TO LAS VEGAS.

[Correspondent of the Missouri Democrat.]
LAS VEGAS, NEW MEXICO, Nov. 18, 1859.

Editors Missouri Democrat—…Our next day's travel brought us to the village of Parowan. This place contains a population of near 1000 souls, and is by far the most prosperous Mormon settlement in the Territory. We were treated with every kindness by the people of the village, and left the next morning with the sincere regret that there were so few like them in the God-forsaken territory of Utah. Our fifth day's travel brought us to the famous Mountain Meadows. During the day we passed through Cedar City, which, from a thriving settlement of about 2000 souls, has dwindled away till scarce 300 remain. The entire male portion of the inhabitants of this place participated in the massacre of the Arkansas emigrant train, on the 10th of September, 1857,[1] and since that dark and bloody day, the curse of God seems to have settled upon the place, and many have fled it, fearing the ghosts of the murdered victims.[2] We walked over the ground and visited the different spots where the different acts of the tragedy were perpetrated, and our eyes, though unused to the melting mood, filled with tears as we gazed upon the scattered remnants of the victims that lay strewn over the plain. Our first visit was to the ravine where one hundred and fourteen women and children were shot down by their ruthless enemies. Here we picked up several bunches of hair that had belonged to the murdered ones….

Civilian & Telegraph, Cumberland, Maryland, January 19, 1860, pg. 1

SUICIDES.—The New York Times says:—Of the twenty-six cases of suicide that we record this morning, eleven were accomplished by hanging, six by the use of the razor or knife, six by poisoning, and three by drowning. The alleged cause in six

---

[1] The Mountain Meadows Massacre occurred on September 11, 1857, when Utah Territorial Militia killed 120-140 members of the Baker-Fancher wagon train as part of the Utah War between American settlers and Mormon settlers in the Utah Territory. All emigrants of the wagon train under the age of seven were slaughtered to prevent witnesses.

[2] The Mountain Meadows Massacre site is considered one of the most haunted sites in Utah. Visitors have reported hearing screams and the sound of crying at the site.

cases was insanity, in two rum, one victim by a letter found in his pocket, charged his reputable wife with his ruin; one lately widowed, was living with a lewd woman, and his pure wife's ghost haunted him....

The Pacific Commercial Advertiser, Honolulu, Hawaiian Islands, February 16, 1860, pg. 3

They have started a ghost near Sonora, California. Some miners lodging in a barn were frightened off by an appearance in the shape of a huge man, about sixteen feet high, who arose from amidst the hay piled up in the barn, and tossed the bales around as if they were light as feathers in his grasp. On one occasion one of the men fired at the ghost, but the ball had no effect.

> They have started a ghost near Sonora, California. Some miners lodging in barn were frightened off by an appearance in the shape of a huge man, about sixteen feet high, who arose from amidst the hay piled up in the barn, and tossed the bales around as if they were light as feathers in his grasp. On one occasion one of the men fired at the ghost, but the ball had no effect.

The Penny Press, Cincinnati, Ohio, February 17, 1860, pg. 1.

THE CONNECTICUT GHOST AGAIN.—The Fair Haven ghost still continues to frighten nocturnal travelers, and the thing has got to such a pass that several Fair Haven gentlemen, whose business leads them to walk home from New Haven at night, now go around with a Colt's revolver, and mean to put a bullet in the ghost the first opportunity.

Daily Dispatch, Richmond, Virginia,
February 21, 1860, pg. 1.

SEARCHING FOR A PIRATE'S GOLD.—The Taunton (Mass.) Gazette says that two men of that town are engaged in digging on the northeast side of Foolish Hill, in Foxboro', as they say, under the direction of spirits, in search of treasures alleged to have been buried in that place by one John Bernard,[3] a pirate and highwayman. One of the diggers asserts that he actually saw the ghost of the deceased pirate near the place where these operations are now going on, and both appear to be full in the faith that something valuable will reward their toil. Hundreds of people have already visited the spot, and the labors of these simpletons are watched with interest by great numbers

The Portage County Democrat, Ravenna, Ohio,
February 22, 1860, pg. 1.
From *the Boston Traveler.*

A GHOST STORY—OR, 'SECOND SIGHT.' —Mr. Hector McDonald, of Canada, was recently on a visit to Boston. When he left home his family were enjoying good health, and he anticipated a pleasant journey. The second morning after his arrival at Boston, when leaving his bed to dress for breakfast, he saw reflected in a mirror the corpse of a woman lying in the bed from which he had just risen. Spell bound, he gazed with intense feeling and tried to recognize the features of the corpse, but in vain; he could not even move his eyelids; he felt deprived of action, for how long he knew not. He was at last started by the

---

[3] John Bernard (1756-1828) was an English actor; he was not a pirate or highwayman. In 1797, while sailing to Boston, Massachusetts the actor's ship encountered pirates off of the coast of the Azores. For more information of this incident see http://www.newenglandhistoricalsociety.com/john-bernard-18th-century-comedian-dodges-pirates/ (accessed August 11, 2018).

ringing of a bell for breakfast, and sprang to the bed to satisfy himself if what he had seen reflected in the mirror was real or an illusion. He found the bed as [he] had left it; he looked again into the mirror, but only saw the bed truly reflected. During the day he thought much upon the illusion, and determined next morning to rub his eyes and feel perfectly sure that he was wide awake before he left the bed. But, notwithstanding these precautions, the vision was repeated, with this addition, that he thought he recognized in the corpse some resemblance to the features of his wife.

In the course of the day he received a letter from his wife, in which she stated that she was quite well, and hoped he was enjoying himself among his friends. As he was devotedly attached to her, and always anxious for her safety, he supposed that his morbid fears had conjured up the vision he had seen reflected in the glass, and went about his business as cheerful as usual. On the morning of the third day, after he had dressed, he found himself in thought in his own house, leaning over the coffin of his wife. His friends were assembled, the minister was performing the funeral services, his children wept—he was in the house of death. He followed the corpse to the grave; he heard the earth rumble upon the coffin, he saw the grave filled, and the green sods covered over it, yet by some strange power, he could see through the ground the entire form of his wife as she lay in her coffin.

He looked in the faces of those around him, but no one seemed to notice him; he tried to weep, but the tears refused to flow; his very heart felt as hard as a rock. Enraged at his own want of feeling, he determined to throw himself upon the grave and lie there till his heart should break, when he was recalled to consciousness by a friend, who entered the room to inform him that breakfast was ready. He started as if awoke from a profound sleep, though he was standing before the mirror with a hair brush in his hand.

After composing himself, he related to his friends what he had seen, and both concluded that a good breakfast only was wanting to dissipate his unpleasant reflections. A few days afterwards, however, he received the melancholy intelligence that his wife had died suddenly, and the time corresponded with the day he had been startled by the first vision in the mirror. When he returned home, he described minutely all the details of the funeral he had seen in his vision, and they corresponded with the facts. This is probably one of the most vivid instances of clairvoyance on record. Mr. M'Donald knows nothing of modern spiritualism or clairvoyance, as most of his life has been passed upon a farm and among forests. It may not be amiss to state that his father, who was a Scotch Highlander, had the gift of 'second sight.'

New Orleans Daily Crescent, New Orleans, Louisiana, February 28, 1860, pg. 1.

A GHOST THROWING BRICKBATS.—Quite a shower of brickbats[4] and other missiles were thrown out, on Sunday, by some concealed occupant of the famous old "haunted house" in the Fourth District. One of the missiles struck a miss who was passing, and straightway the police got after the ghost, and caught it. It was a vagrantish masculine ghost, answering to the earthly name of Bill Perkins alias Mob Town, alias Chips; a regular holy ghost, so far as its clothing was concerned. Recorder Adams will exorcise it soon.

The Hillsdale Standard, Hillsdale, Michigan, March 6, 1860, pg. 2.
From *the Cleveland Herald.*

A SINGULAR STORY.—A remarkable story is current in Pittsburgh, and other parts of Western Pennsylvania. It possesses the elements of the wildest romance, but is religiously believed by very many persons. We give it as it was told to us, without, of course, endorsing the occurrences as actual facts.

About two weeks ago, in the village of Latrobe, in Western Pennsylvania, a solemn mass was observed in the Roman Catholic Church, for the repose of the soul of a dead priest. A number of worshipers were in the church at the time. Just as the officiating priest was about to perform the most solemn part of the rites, his purpose was checked by an astonishing appearance. The form of

---

[4] Brickbats are a piece of brick used as a weapon.

the deceased priest himself appeared in front of the altar, with hands uplifted in a warning manner. The officiating clergyman stepped back when the ghostly priest, or priestly ghost, addressed his brother in the flesh and the congregation. He said they were taking unnecessary trouble to get him out of Purgatory. The Priest might save his prayers and the penitents their pennies.—They could not get him out of Purgatory because he was never in it. Furthermore, there was no chance for him to get there, as there never was such a place as Purgatory. It was all a mistake. He should feel very much obliged if they could get him out of the spot where he was, but that was impossible. There was but two places of future existence—one was perpetual bliss, and the other of perpetual punishment. *Only two priests ever went to Heaven*—and he was not one of them.—He therefore warned them that their masses for the repose of his or any other defunct person's soul, where useless.

With that motion this remarkable ghost disappeared, and the sacred congregation dispersed.

Vᴼᴸ. XV.   WASHINGTON, D. C., TUESDAY, MARCH 6, 1860.   Nᴼ. 2,199.

Evening Star, Washington, D.C., March 6, 1860, pg. 1. From *The Pittsburg Dispatch*.

A Strange Story.
THE GHOST OF A BENEDICTINE MONK APPEARS TO A NOVICE—TIDINGS FROM PURGATORY.

We alluded recently to a current report that the apparition of a priest had appeared to the living at Latrobe; and we present below a detailed account of this supernatural phenomenon, in which the exaggerations of the current rumors are corrected, and the reality of the appearance affirmed. After all, there is nothing more marvelous in this than in the stories related in "Mrs. Crow's Night Side of Nature"[5] and Owen's "Footfalls on the Boundaries of Another World,"[6] while it is better authenticated than half of the narratives admitted into those volumes of the supermundane. Those, therefore, who are ready to subscribe to the truth of the narrations given by Owen—who, himself, has come to believe in an intermediate state of progression—will be sadly puzzled upon what grounds to discord the Benedictine Monk of St. Vincent's Abbey, as an illusion. The following is the communication of the worthy Abbot:

> **A Strange Story.**
> THE GHOST OF A BENEDICTINE MONK APPEARS TO A NOVICE—TIDINGS FROM PURGATORY.
> [From the Pittsburgh Dispatch.]
> We alluded recently to a current report that the apparition of a priest had appeared to the living at Latrobe; and we present below a detailed account of this supernatural phenomenon, in which the exaggerations of the current rumors are corrected, and the reality of the appearance affirmed. After all, there is nothing more marvelous in this than in the stories related in "Mrs. Crow's Night Side of Nature" and Owen's "Footfalls on the Boundaries of Another World," while it is better authenticated than half of the narratives admitted into those volumes of the supermundane. Those, therefore, who are ready to subscribe to the truth of the narrations given by Owen—who, himself, has come to believe in an intermediate state of progression—will be sadly puzzled upon what grounds to discard the Benedictine Monk of St. Vincent's Abbey, as an illusion. The following is the communication of the worthy Abbot:

EDITORS DISPATCH—*Dear Sirs:*—A friend of mine handed me a copy of the Dispatch of the 25th instant, drawing my attention to a "Queer Story," telling that recently, while "Mass" was being celebrated in Latrobe, the spirit of some priest or saint appeared and communicated the information to the assembly that it was all a misapprehension about "Purgatory," no such place of intermediate state of probation existing; and worse than all, that but two priests had yet found their way to Heaven.

The truth is, that at St. Vincent's Abbey,[7] near Latrobe, a Novice saw, from the 18th Sept. until the 19th Nov. 1859, every

---

[5] *The Night Side of Nature: Or, Ghosts and Ghost Seers* by Catherine Crowe (1803-1876).

[6] *Footfalls on the Boundaries of another World* by Robert Dale Owen (1801-1877).

[7] The Archabbey of St. Vincent's was founded in 1846 as the first Benedictine monastery in the United States.

day, from eleven to twelve o'clock, a.m., or from twelve to two o'clock in the night, the apparition of a Benedictine Monk in his full festival dress. After all, he asked him, in the presence of another member of the order, what he wanted. The spirit then answered that he had been suffering seventy-seven years already, because he had not said seven Masses of obligation; that he had appeared to seven other Benedictines, at different times, and had not been heard; and that he would have to appear after eleven years again, if he would not help him. He wanted the seven Masses said for him, besides this the Novice should, for seven days, observe the strictest silence and retreat; and more, he should say for thirty-three days, each day three times, the "Fiftieth Psalm" barefooted and his arms stretched out.

This was done from the 21st November till the 25th December, when the last Mass was celebrated, and the ghost disappeared. During this time he had appeared several times again, exhorted the Novice most impressively, to pray for the Souls in Purgatory, since they suffer very hard, and consequently are very thankful to those who concur to their redemption; and, sad enough, said that of the five Priests who had already died at the Abbey, no one was yet in Heaven, but suffering in Purgatory.

This is in substance the facts that gave origin to your strange report; we give it as much credit as it deserves; but this report is correct.

B. WIMER, Abbot.
St. Vincent's Abbey, 26th Feb., 1860.

The Press and Tribune, Chicago, Illinois,
March 8, 1860, **pg.** 2.
From *the Pittsburgh Chronicle.*

THE PRIESTLY GHOST AGAIN
Corrected Statement of his Opinions.

Some days since a paragraph appeared in one of our contemporaries, to the effect that the apparition of a priest had appeared to certain persons in Latrobe, and stated, among other things, that there was no such place as purgatory, and that but two priests had yet found their way to Heaven. A letter from the Superior of St. Vincent's Abbey contradicts to a certain extent the language attributed to the defunct clergyman, but admits that his ghostship did make his appearance, and had several interviews with one of the inmates of the institution....

The above coming from an Abbot, is decidedly rich, and throws the celebrated Cock Lane ghost[8] completely into the shade. For our part, we believe the letter of "Mr. Wimer" to be a forgery of the most impudent character. Our reasons for arriving at this conclusion are easily explained: The Abbot spells his name "Wimmer,"[9] instead of "Wimer," as it appears as published, and is altogether too sensible a man to ventilate such a silly story as the above. We think when the whole matter comes to be investigated about that "Mr. Wimer" will be found as much of a myth as the "Benedictine Ghost."

Evening Star, Washington, D.C., March 12, 1860, pg. 1.

A GHOST SIXTEEN FEET HIGH.—The following ghost story is solemnly related by the editor of the Sonora (Cal.) Age, who claims to have seen the "what is it?"

"Lyon's Ranch, near Sonora, is haunted. The place was once the property of James Lyons, who assassinated one of the Blackly brothers, some months ago, after having sold the ranch to them. The shade is presumed to belong to the murdered brother, Blackly. The barn seems to be the principal scene of its operations, and a number of miners who slept there have been driven from their lodgings by its remarkable pranks. According to their story, it appeared to them in the shape of a huge man about

---

[8] The Cock Lane Ghost occurred in London, England in 1762, it was later determined to be a hoax.

[9] Archabbott Boniface Wimmer, O.S.B. (1809-1887) founded the Archabbey of St. Vincent's in 1846.

sixteen feet high, who arose from amidst the hay piled up in the barn and tossed the bales around as if they were light as feathers in his grasp.

"The story goes that this unwelcome visitor on several occasions chased the lodgers from the barn, making giant strides after the fugitives. On one occasion one of the men shot at the ghost, but the ball had no effect. The upshot of the story is that his ghostship remains master of the field—or, rather the barn."

New-York Daily Tribune, New York, New York, March 13, 1860, pg. 6.
From *The Evening Post*.

NEW FOOTFALLS FROM ANOTHER WORLD.

THE ASTOR LIBRARY VISITED BY A GHOST—THE LIBRARIAN AND THE GHOST HAVE THREE INTERVIEWS—GHOSTLY TASTES IN LITERATURE— DEMONOLOGY AND WITCHCRAFT.

For several days past there has been a bit of personal gossip afloat up-town which, as in all similar instances, has been highly exaggerated. Yet even allowing for three exaggerations, the facts or the suppositions—which ever they be—as related by one of the principle actors, are of themselves strange enough to satisfy the most inveterate admirer of the marvelous; and as the story has been solemnly asseverated before a mixed company of some twenty persons, and after-ward retailed and repeated so much as to be almost the town talk, we are committing no impropriety, we trust, in stating the circumstances, as far as we have been able to discover them.

The numerous literary persons and others who frequent the spacious halls of the Astor Library[10] will be interested, therefore, in learning that their favorite retreat is haunted. Of course, on seeing the comfortable, well lighted rooms in the day-time, when filled with careful readers, and enlivened often by the presence of gaily dressed lady and other visitors, nothing seems more preposterous than the idea of ghosts. But let the reader imagine these wide halls as they are at night, swathed in darkness, the gloomy alcoves casting yet deeper and gloomier shadows—when a footfall reverberates through the wide expanse with mysterious echoes, and when the lamp borne by the startled explorer along torturous passages and among musty tomes sends a feeble ray, that scarcely serves to make the darkness visible, and the aspect is very different. At this time the Astor Library—and, for that matter, all large libraries at such a time—is a rather dismal place, and suggests, unpleasantly enough, to any one who may be there alone, Hood's lines:

> "O'er all there hung a shadow and a fear,
> A sense of mystery the spirited daunted,
> Which said, as plain as whisper in the ear,
> The place is haunted."[11]

It was as such a time, in such a place and to one lonely explorer, that the ghost of the Astor Library appeared.

To understand the circumstances of this remarkable apparition the more fully, the reader should remember that Dr. Cogswell,[12] the efficient librarian, has been for some time engaged in the compilation of a complete catalogue of the library. Although over a year since it was commenced, the work has only reached to the letter P. Dr. Cogswell is an unmarried man, and

---

[10] Astor Library opened in 1854 as a free public library. In 1895 the Astor Library consolidated with the Lenox Library and the Tilden Foundation to become the New York Public Library.

[11] "The Haunted House. A Romance" by Thomas Hood (1799-1845) in *The Poetical Works of Thomas Hood* (Boston: Philips, Sampson and Company, 1857).

[12] Dr. Joseph Cogswell (1786-1871) co-founded the Astor Library with John Jacob Astor.

occupies a sleeping apartment in the upper part of the library, the janitor residing in the basement. It is the rule of the library to dismiss visitors at sunset, and during the evening and night no individual beside Dr. Cogswell and the janitor and his family remain in the building.

Against the advice of his friends, Dr. Cogswell devotes hours of night that should be given to repose to the pursuance of his work on the catalogue. Naturally anxious to hasten forward its completion, and fired with all the enthusiasm of a professed bibliopole, his labours in this tedious and difficult task are almost incredible. At the same time the work is of that dry statistical character which is by no means suggestive of fanciful apparitions, nor is the indefatigable complier a man easily swayed by the passing delusions of the eye or brain.

South Hall of the Astor Library, from Harper's Weekly, Supplement, October 2, 1875

Some two weeks ago, Dr. Cogswell was at work as usual on the catalogue. It was about 11 o'clock at night, and having occasion to refer to some books in a distant part of the library, he left his desk, took his candle, and, as he had often done before, pursued his cause among the winding passages toward the desired spot. But before reaching it, while in an alcove in the south-west part of the

NEW FOOTFALLS FROM ANOTHER WORLD.

From The Evening Post.

THE ASTOR LIBRARY VISITED BY A GHOST—THE LIBRARIAN AND THE GHOST HAVE THREE INTERVIEWS—GHOSTLY TASTES IN LITERATURE—DEMONOLOGY AND WITCHCRAFT.

For several days past there has been a bit of personal gossip afloat up-town which, as in all similar instances, has been highly exaggerated. Yet even allowing for these exaggerations, the facts or the suppositions—which ever they be—as related by one of the principal actors, are of themselves strange enough to satisfy the most inveterate admirer of the marvelous; and as the story has been solemnly asseverated before a mixed company of some twenty persons, and afterward retailed and repeated to much as to be almost the town talk, we are committing no impropriety, we trust, in stating the circumstances, as far as we have been able to discover them.

older portion of the building, he was startled by seeing a man, respectably dressed in citizen's clothes, surveying a shelf of books. The doctor supposed it to be a robber who had secreted himself for the purpose of abstracting some of the valuable works in the library; after stepping back behind a partition for a moment, he again moved cautiously forward to catch a glimpse of the individual's face, when to his surprise he recognized in the supposed robber the features of a physician (whose name we forbear giving) who had lived in the immediate vicinity of the library, and who had died some six weeks ago! It should be bourne in mind that the deceased person was a mere casual acquaintance of Dr. Cogswell, not an intimate friend, and since his death Dr. Cogswell had not thought of him.

But the apparition was in the presence of a man not easily scared. The Librarian so far from fainting or shrieking, as might reasonably be expected, calmly addressed the ghost:

"Dr.—," said he, "you seldom, if ever, visited this Library while living. Why do you trouble us now when dead?"

Perhaps the ghost did not like the sound of the human voice; anyway, it gave no answer, but disappeared.

The next day Mr. Cogswell thought over the matter, attributed it to some optical delusion, and in the evening proceeded with his work as usual. Again he wished to refer to some books, and again visited the south-western alcove. There again, as large as life, was the ghost, very calmly and placidly surveying the shelves. Mr. Cogswell again spoke to it:

"Dr.—," said he, "again I ask you, why you who never visited the Library while living, trouble it now when dead?"

Again the ghost vanished, and the undaunted librarian pursued his task without interruption. The next day he examined the shelves before which the apparition had been seen standing, and by a singular coincidence, found that they were filled with books devoted to demonology, witchcraft, magic, spiritualism, & c. Some of these books are rare tomes, several centuries old, written in Latin, illustrated with quaint diagrams, and redolent of mysticism; while on the next shelves are their young brethren, the neat spruce works of modern spiritualists, of Brittan, Davis, Edmonds, and others. The very titles on these mystic books are suggestive. There are the Prophecies or Prognostications of Michael Nostradamus,[13] a folio published in London in 1672; Albamasor de Conjectionibus; Kerner's Majiken; Godwin's Lives of the Necromancers;[14] Glanvil on Witches and Apparitions;[15] Cornelius Agrippa;[16] Bodin's Demonomania;[17] Lilly's Astrology[18] and others, a perusal of any of which would effectually murder the sleep of a person of ordinary nerves for at least half a dozen nights. It was these volumes that appeared to attract the apparition.

The third night, Mr. Cogswell, still determined that the shade, spirit, delusion or effect of indigestion—whatever it might be—should not interfere with the duties, again visited the various books to which he wished to refer to, and when occasion demanded, did not fail to approach the mystic alcove. There again

---

[13] Michel de Nostredame (1503-1566) was a French seer and mystic.

[14] *Lives of the Necromancers: Or An Account of the Most Eminent Persons in Successive Ages Who Have Claimed for Themselves or To Whom Has Been Imputed by Others the Exercise of Magical Powers* (1834) by William Godwin (1756-1836).

[15] *Saducismus Triumphatus* (1681) by Joseph Glanvill (1636-1680).

[16] Cornelius Agrippa (1486-1535) was a German writer on the occult.

[17] *Of the Demon-mania of the Sorcerers* (1580) by Jean Bodin (1530-1596).

[18] William Lilly (1602-1681) was an English astrologer.

was the apparition, dressed precisely as before, in a gentleman's usual costume, as natural as life, and with a hand raised, as if about to take down a book. Mr. Cogswell again spoke—

"Dr.—," he said boldly. "This is the third time I have met you. Tell me if any of this class of books now disturb you? If they do, I will have them removed."

But the ungrateful ghost, without acknowledging this accommodating spirit on the part of its interrogator, disappeared. Nor has it been seen since, and the librarian has continued his nightly researches since without interruption.

A few days ago at a dinner party at the house of a well-known wealthy gentleman, Mr. Cogswell related the circumstances as above recorded, as nearly as we can learn. As some 18 or 20 people were present, the remarkable story of course was soon spread about. A number of literary men, including an eminent historian and others, heard the recital, and though they attribute Mr. Cogswell's ghost seeing to the strain and tension of his nerves during his too protracted labors at the catalogue, they yet confess that the story has its remarkable phases. Both Mr. Cogswell and the deceased physician were persons of a practical turn of mind, and always treated the marvelous ghost stories sometimes set afloat with deserved contempt. And, as they were not at all intimate, it will be at least a curious question for the psychologist to determine, why the idea of this deceased gentleman should come to Mr. Cogswell's brain and resolve itself into an apparition, when engaged in dry, statistical labors, which should effectually banish all thoughts of the marvelous.

Acting on the advice of several friends, Mr. Cogswell is now absent on a short trip to Charleston to recuperate his energies. His indefatigable industry, his devotion to the interests of the Library, and his great efficiency as a librarian, render it highly desirable that he should enjoy recreation and repose, and not endanger his health by a too close application to his duties. In regard to the apparition we will make no comments, but give the story as related by Dr. Cogswell, as we are credibly informed, and as it has already been talked about in various literary and domestic circles in this city.

Evening Star, Washington, D.C., March 15, 1860, pg. 1.

A GHOST APPARITION RESPONSIBLE FOR THE NON-PAYMENT OF RENT.—A day or two since one of the oldest constables of the city was employed to serve an ejectment writ upon a shoemaker residing in an alley-way running from Congress street. The man, who is of Irish extraction, but of intelligent appearance, declared to the officer that he did not pay the rent because the house wasn't tenantable. "And why not?" said the officer; "it appears to be in good repair." "That's not it," said the tenant; "sure a house is not tenantable that's haunted." "Haunted said the officer; "you're talking foolishly." "It's myself that's seen him," said Pat; "he walks at night; and the last tenant couldn't stand it, and had to pack up and leave." Pat explained further that a man had died suddenly in another part of the house some years back, and his ghost had ever since been about the premises. Pat called his son, a boy of tender years, who corroborated his father's story about the ghost, which he had also seen under the closet, looking like a dead man. Thus the matter stands at present. The ghost, it seems, however, is not powerful enough to drive the tenant out, and the courts will have to issue a mandate of ejectment. As for Pat, before he leaves he is determined, as he says, to know the "bottom of the matter."—*Boston Traveller, March 8.*

The Press and Tribune, Chicago, Illinois, March 16, 1860, pg. 1.
Correspondent of the Press and Tribune.

OUR NEW YORK LETTER.
The Ghost at the Astor Library…

New York, March 13, 1860—Everybody has heard of the Astor Library, with its one hundred thousand volumes of all ages, languages and nations—it's stately alcoves, curious manuscripts, and magnificent folios—it's unequalled facilities for students, compilers and bibliophilists. Everyone, also, who knows the venerable, scholastic Dr. Joseph G. Cogswell, librarian of the institution, who collected in Europe and elsewhere the volumes under his charge, knows that he is one of the most cool and dispassionate men alive; one who, among a thousand, would be the least likely to have his sound judgment carried away by his imagination, or to indulge in telling any romantic story that he did not believe to be strictly true.

The Doctor is consequently [a] high authority in Manhattan on all matters past, present or to come.

And the Doctor declares that he has seen a ghost. Moreover, the ghost in question haunts the Astor Library.

Only a select few, who frequent the Historical Society or Century Club,[19] have known the facts until to-day. It seems that about a month ago, an old physician, by the name of Sands, with whom the Doctor was well acquainted, found that his "sands of life had run out"—in short, died, at his residence in Lafayette Place, nearly adjacent to the Library building. Deceased was remarkable rather for his acquaintance with the mysteries of calomel[20] and jalop,[21] than for his literary tendencies; was much better known at the cliniques[22] than among the bookworms. Dr. Cogswell has a room in the Astor Library, where he sleeps o'nights, and from whence, with true scholastic ardor, he often emerges in the silent midnight watches, to roam about among the beloved books, and perhaps study out some knotty reference, which the press of visitors prevents him from pursuing during the day. He was thus engaged one night, two weeks since, without a thought in his head of the crusty old Esculapian,[23] whom he knew to have been safely deposited under ground some time before, and supposed himself to be entirely alone, when he was surprised at seeing a person uneasily moving through the distant alcoves. The Doctor went straight up to his nocturnal visitor, and was astonished at beholding the features of his deceased acquaintance—old Mr. Sands!...

---

[19] The Century Club was founded in 1829 by William Cullen Bryant to promote the fine arts and literature.

[20] Calomel was used as a purgative.

[21] Jalop was used as a purgative.

[22] Clinics

[23] Healer

THE NEW YORK HERALD.

The New York Herald, New York, New York,
March 17, 1860, pg. 10
From the Daily News

THE GHOSTS IN THE HISTORICAL SOCIETY BUILDING.

As the policemen were taking their customary nap in the doorway of the Historical Society last night, they were awakened by strange noises within. On going to the sidewalk and looking up at the bust of Herodotus,[24] it was observed to nod and wink in a significant manner. Greatly alarmed, they aroused the janitor, who, on examination, found the Nineveh Marbles performing a quadrille,[25] King Nisroch[26] having mounted the table as floor manager. On ascending higher, they found that the Chiriqui[27] idols had attacked the mummies used at Mr. Prime's lecture, and threatened their destruction, they being unable to defend themselves in consequence of the swathing cloths which confined their arms. But they were talking loudly and rapidly, evidently hinting what would happen if their arms were at liberty. This is a strong proof of the warlike spirit of the ancient patriarchs. One of the policemen uttered a pious exclamation, the noise suddenly ceased, and everything resumed its former condition. We are unable to give any explanation of this wonderful affair, although it is rumored (probably without foundation) that the paper on Witchcraft, read before the Society last week, was the cause of it. If anything else happens, we shall report in due season.[28]

---

[24] Herodotus (c. 484 BC-c. 425 BC) was a Greek historian.
[25] The quadrille was a popular form of square dancing during the 19th-century.
[26] Assyrian god mentioned in the Bible.
[27] Chiriqui is a province in Panama.
[28] This article is an example of the parody pieces frequently found in 19th-century American newspapers.

THE DAILY EXCHANGE.

VOL. V—NO. 616.   BALTIMORE, TUESDAY, MARCH 27, 1860.   PRICE TWO CENTS.

The Daily Exchange, Baltimore, Maryland,
March 27, 1860, pg. 1.

THE ASTOR LIBRARY GHOSTS.—Some of the New Yorkers think it rather hard that the library should be open to ghosts in the evening and closed against living flesh and blood. As Mr. Astor designed his benefaction chiefly for the denizens of this earth, it is claimed that they ought to have an equal chance with ghosts. The claim seems to be reasonable.

THE ASTOR LIBRARY GHOSTS.—Some of the New Yorkers think it rather hard that the library should be open to ghosts in the evening and closed against living flesh and blood. As Mr. Astor designed his benefaction chiefly for the denizens of this earth, it is claimed that they ought to have an equal chance with ghosts. The claim seems to be reasonable.

The Independent Press, Abbeville, South Carolina,
March 30, 1860, pg. 4.

An author, ridiculing the idea of ghosts, asks how a dead man can get into a locked room. Probable with a skeleton-key.

Cincinnati Daily Press.

VOL. III, NO. 38.   CINCINNATI, WEDNESDAY MORNING, APRIL 4, 1860.   PRICE ONE CENT.

Cincinnati Daily Press, Cincinnati, Ohio,
April 4, 1860, pg. 1.

A "GHOST' THRASHED BY A WOMAN.—The Lafayette (Ind.) *Courier* tells an amusing story of a company of young ladies and gentlemen of that place who took it into their heads to adjourn from a social party to a walk near the cemetery. As they approached the ghostly place a lady screamed. All eyes turned to the point indicated by her alarm, and saw a ghost coming towards them, appareled in orthodox white. They all ran, but one sturdy woman of the strong-minded class, who stood her ground till the ghost got to her, when she seized it, and thrashed out his frightened disguise a mischievous fellow who had heard the project of walking about the grave-yard discussed, and hid himself there to give the party a fright. She led him back to the house, and in reply to the questions that poured upon her, said: "Can't fool me, I've seen too many men in sheets to get frightened at them!"

Doubtless she had; but we question if she treated the other fellows so harshly as the chap in the cemetery.

Alexandria Gazette, Alexandria, VA, April 6, 1860, pg. 2.

THE ASTOR LIBRARY GHOST.—Burleigh, the New York correspondent of the Boston Journal, in his last letter to that paper, writes:—Dr. Johnson[29] said—"Say that a house in London has the plague, and all in London will go and see it." I have spent a few days at the Astor Library. It is quite amusing to see the crowds that drift in to see the place where Dr. Cogswell saw the ghost of Dr. Post. Ladies, especially, come in in couples, in fours, alone and with male attendants; with a soft tread and an awe in their looks, with a trembling voice, they step from alcove to alcove, as if they thought the form of the spirit would start out and greet them. And when the Doctor is seen behind the counter (for he has come back), the small talk runs—"There, that is he," "there he is"—showing how deeply the public mind is interested in the story of the haunted library, and proving that, after all that has been said and written on the matter, men as readily believe in the

---

[29] Dr. Samuel Johnson (1709-1784) was an English writer, poet, essayist and lexicographer.

existence of ghosts to-day as they did eighteen hundred years ago, when the disciples thought their Lord was only a spirit.

Burlington Free Press, Burlington, Vermont, April 20, 1860, pg. 3.

A SPIRITUAL INQUIRY.—Is it likely that ghosts talk in the dead languages?

The Press and Tribune, Chicago, Illinois, April 20, 1860, pg. 3.

The Ghost of the Astor Library.
The New York Correspondent of the New Orleans

Picayune, "H. F.," (Belle Brittan) is responsible for this bit of gossip:

The "Astor Library Ghost Story: is one of the most talked-of and laughed-at topics of the day. My own theory is, that we all see ghosts in dreams, and that the venerable Dr. Cogswell was dreaming when he saw the late Dr. Sands standing before the "Demonology Alcove," in the Library. I know a most intelligent and accomplished lady who has seldom slept for the last seven years without being visited by a phantom in the shape of a man, handsome and more agreeable than any other gentleman she had ever seen with her waking eyes; and although at first she was frightened at his advances; she now finds in the delightful nightly interviews the chief charm of life.

This dream phantom makes love like an angel. The lady is finely organized and of a highly nervous temperament, and the excitement of this ghostly intercourse is exhausting her physical life. Every day her cheeks grow paler and thinner; and her eyes brighter and larger. I presume this strange experience, which was confided to me as a profound and precious secret, with many minute and most interesting particulars, is by no means peculiar to my fair friend.

Doubtless this publication of the fact will develop many similar instances, just as the publication of Mrs. Crowe's and Robert Dale Owen's Ghost Stories have called forth thousands more of the some sort. In this sad world of trouble and vexation of spirit, I doubt there are but few of us unsatisfied mortals in dreams—in sacred visits from the dead—in blissful meetings with the living.

> "And even in dream to be blessed,
> Is so sweet that I ask for no more."[30]

To return to Dr. Cogswell. He was overworked and weary. The body slept, and he saw, in his "mind's eye," one whom he recognized as dead, and questioned him as to his departed spirit. He woke, and his vision vanished. In his somnambulism[31] he had moved from his desk to a certain alcove. Volia tout![32] The only surprising thing about the matter is that so sensible a man as Dr. Cogswell should have related the circumstances at a large dinner party as a ghost story, and not as a dream. But he is an old man, verging on fourscore years; and it is written, "Your old men shall see visions; and your young men shall dream dreams."[33]

NEW ORLEANS DAILY CRESCENT.

PUBLISHED EVERY DAY, SUNDAY EXCEPTED, BY J. O. NIXON, AT No. 70 CAMP STREET.

VOLUME XIII.   THURSDAY MORNING, APRIL 26, 1860.   NUMBER 45.

New Orleans Daily Crescent, New Orleans, Louisiana, April 26, 1860, pg. 1.

---

[30] "Though 'Tis All But a Dream" in *The Prose and Poetry of Europe and America: Consisting of Literary Gems and Curiosities* compiled by G.P. Morris and N.P. Willis (New York: Leavitt & Allen, 1845), 399.
[31] Sleepwalking
[32] French for "That's all."
[33] Acts 2:17.

STRANGE GHOSTS IN THE HAUNTED HOUSE.— Of course everybody in town has seen the ruined and isolated old Spanish mansion, which stands by itself in the midst of a large square ground at the corner of Tchoupitoulas and Washington street;

STRANGE GHOSTS IN THE HAUNTED HOUSE.—Of course everybody in town has seen the ruined and isolated old Spanish mansion, which stands by itself in the midst of a large square of ground at the corner of Tchoupitoulas and Washington streets; and everybody, more or less, has read some of the various sketches and novelettes, which the appearance and history of the old ruin have evoked from the brains and pens of some of our local poets and fanciful sketch-writers. The building has for years done earthly service enough in affording shelter to cows and Irish washerwomen in its lower part, and to bats and drunken vagrants in its upper part. All sorts of an institution is this "haunted house," to begin with.

and everybody, more or less, has read some of the various sketches and novelettes, which the appearance and history of the old ruin have evoked from the brains and pens of some of our local poets and fanciful sketch-writers.[34]   The building has for years done earthly service enough in affording shelter to cows and Irish washerwomen in its lower part, and to bats and drunken vagrants in its upper part. All sorts of an institution is this "haunted house," to begin with.

On Saturday night last, the house was haunted by several ghosts in the most extraordinary manner. Whether the two principal ghosts had formerly inhabited the place, and know more of it than the common run of ghosts, or whether they had been drawn to the spot by the reading of "The Haunted, by Charles Howard," is a question which must forever remain unsettled.

The third, or insignificant ghost, was the first to appear in the haunted house on Saturday night last. He is well known, in the flesh, to most people in the Fourth District; a ghost very fond of the coffee-houses; somewhat addicted to taking too many flies in his lemonade, and very fond of sleeping off his liquor in the old haunted house, because it is quiet, well ventilated, and rent free.

Toward midnight this ghost had snored off so much of his alcohol, that a subdued sort of noise in the lower story put on an

---

[34] This house was known as the Livaudais Plantation and was known as the "Haunted House of Lafayette." The plantation house was torn down in 1863. See "Holiday Tour Set For Garden District" by Samuel Wilson, Jr. in *Preservation*, Vol. 6, No. 9, pg. 1.
http://prcno.org/programs/preservationinprint/piparchives/1979%20PIP/December%201979/0.html. (accessed August 11, 2018).

end to his slumber. Startled, he rose cautiously and went to the old rickety stairway, from beneath which he could see the light of flickering candles, and hear a sound as of men delving deeply into the bowels of the earth. His curiosity tempted him to steal down far enough to lean over and peep under the stairway. He looked, and he saw, to his great horror, two of the most terrible ghosts that could have possibly appeared to him. He recognized them as powerful police ghosts, who would be sure to seize him and spirit him away to the lock-up, if they caught him there, peering in upon their privacy. He remained long enough to see what they were doing.

In their shirt-sleeves, with mattock[35] and shovel, digging deeply into the earth, by the pale light of the candles, the two ghosts bore a very strong resemblance to ordinary Irish laborers; only their faces betrayed them to the scared ghost on the stairway as the well-known police ghosts, Sergeant Hagar and officer Sam Caldwell, the latter once Lieutenant of Police in that end of the town. They were working silently, but like Trojans. The ghost on the stairway, fearful of detection, began stealing up again; but, horror! he was discovered and recognized! "Damn you," said one of the ghosts to him, "If you blow about this, I'll murder you!" Frightened enough, he did not attempt to leave the building, but slunk back into his dark corner upstairs and laid down, though, as a matter of course, he did not sleep.

The ghosts below worked on till nearly daylight, when they stopped, and departed with their mattocks and shovels. The up-stairs ghost afterward left, but not without taking a cautious look to see what the other ghosts had done. They had dug a hole, or well, eight or ten feet deep, and three of four feet wide; a job which kept them hard at work during the greater part of the night.

The up-stairs ghost could not keep still about the matter, though he died for it. He blabbed; and soon the facts of the case were public, that the other ghosts, Hagar and Caldwell, had dug the hole in expectation of finding a fortune of gold or other treasure, which they had their own reasons for believing was buried in the earth, just beneath the old stairway. The story of the recreant ghost is verified well enough by the big pit under the stairway, and the

---

[35] An agricultural tool shaped like a pickax.

freshly-dug dirt heaped around. Some of the dirt has been carried out into daylight by enthusiastic visitors, and carefully examined, have been found.

Any one feeling like buying stock in the Haunted House Placer, or gold diggings, can procure shares very cheap by application to the Messrs. Hagar and Caldwell, who have staked off the claim and established squatter sovereignty over it. Their terms will be, in fact, unusually liberal; for though they are good diggers, they are not Digger Indians.[36]

Alexandria Gazette, Alexandria, VA,
May 5, 1860, pg. 2.

The residents on Duval street, Richmond, Pa., are enjoying a ghost, who throws stones brickbats and glass bottles. The utmost vigilance of the police fails to account for these demonstrations.

The New York Herald, New York, New York,
May 14, 1860, pg. 5.
Brooklyn City News.

A GHOST ARRESTED BY THE POLICE.—For some evening past large crowds of persons gathered in front of St. Ann's church yard, in Fulton street, for the purpose of seeing a ghost, which is was reported made its appearance between the hours of eight and nine o'clock. The sidewalk and street were so densely crowded with spectators on Saturday night, that the police found it necessary to take measures for the purpose of putting an end to the excitement. With this view a policeman took his position within the enclosure, and it was not long before his attention was attracted by an object in white, which hopped about from on grave to another. Watching his opportunity, the officer suddenly appeared to his ghostship, and instead of finding it an apparition without

---

[36] A derogatory term used to describe Native Americans who lived in the Great Basin area of the United States.

substance, discovered the features of a well known citizen whose residence adjoins the graveyard. He was covered with a white sheet, and looked just as a ghost is supposed to look. On being brought outside, the rush became so great that it was with difficulty that Mr. Ghost could be conducted to the station house by the officers. He was arraigned before Captain Smith, who, after advising him of the propriety of discontinuing such practice, permitted him to go. As ghosts are liable to arrest and imprisonment, it is hardly probable that any one will soon again place himself in jeopardy by assuming the character in St. Anne's graveyard.

The Jeffersonian, Stroudsburg, Pennsylvania, May 17, 1860

In Sandusky, Ohio, lives a rich old fellow who has, as is not uncommon, a charming daughter. The maiden loved as maidens will, and, perversely enough, the object of her affection was the wrong man, as the matter was viewed by the father; the latter wished her to marry an elderly man, while her motto was, youth first, and wealth afterward. After unsuccessful attempts to induce her to consent to the unequal nuptials, the stern old progenitor set out in a wagon to procure a magistrate, determined that the wedding should be done at once, and anyhow. In a short time he returned in great fright, went to bed, and had a long fit of sickness. When his strength return[ed], gave him power of continued speech, he explained the mystery by saying that he had seen his wife! It appears that as he was jogging along after the magistrate the ghost of his departed spouse came down from a tree into his vehicle, took the reins from his hand, quietly turned the horse's head and drove her cowed husband back to his home.—Rather than have this thing happen again, he consented to give the daughter to the poor but honest young man, and since then his wife has not harassed him by her unexpected presence or by reminiscences of domestic discipline.

Cincinnati Daily Press, Cincinnati, Ohio,
May 21, 1860, pg. 1.

GHOST EXCITEMENT IN MINNESOTA.—The people of the Third Ward, of St. Paul, are in quite a state of excitement in consequence of a ghost which has appeared to sundry and divers individuals recently, at the bewitching hour of midnight. His ghostship seen on some corner usually near the Park, and steals away noiselessly on being approached, and disappears. It is supposed by some to be Mrs. Bilansky's[37] spirit, as she threatened to haunt the people of St. Paul. Others pooh! pooh! at it, and say it is some one fond of a joke, wrapped in a winding sheet. The police are investigating the subject.

New Orleans Daily Crescent, New Orleans,
Louisiana, May 24, 1860, pg. 1.

A NIGGER GIRL PLAYING GHOST.—Lately an old lady residing on Customhouse street bought a negro girl, who soon

---

[37] Ann Bilansky (c.1820-1860) was executed on March 23, 1860 at Saint Paul, Minnesota, for the murder of her husband Stanislaus Bilansky. She was the first white person executed by hanging in Minnesota. Legend states that Ann Bilansky haunts the cemetery where she is buried looking for her gravestone.

afterward died. Another negro girl in the house spread the report that this girl died of ill-treatment, and affected to be much scandalized when the old lady had a doctor to examine the dead girl's body, with the view of ascertaining the cause of death, and sending in a bill of damage against the party who had sold the girl to her, under guaranty as to her health.

The scandalized wench took an odd method of venting her spite against her mistress. In the first places, she spread the report that her mistress had killed the other girl by torturing her with hot irons; in the second place, she undertook to personate the ghost of the deceased, an invisible ghost; and in this she succeeded in thoroughly alarming her mistress, who was a little inclined to superstition.

One morning, going into the kitchen, the old lady found everything in disorder, fixtures displaced, crockery smashed, etc. The devilish servant girl pretended to be very much alarmed; described the noises she had heard in the night; and maintained that, as no outside person could possibly have got into the kitchen, the author of the damage could have been none other than the dead girl's ghost. The artful wench strengthened her semblance of superstitious fear by "vamosing the ranche" for parts unknown.

The old lady's distress at losing the girl that died was not augmented by this disappearance of her remaining servant. Failing in her inquires after the runaway, she left her description at the police office, with an offer of ten dollars reward for her arrest. Still another and a most alarming distress persecuted the old lady. Strange and startling noises disturbed the stillness of the house, during the ghostly hours of the night; such as an indescribable noise here, a sharp bang there, and a perfect thunder of noise in some other part of the house. The old lady's soul was nearly frightened out of her body.

Night before last, the old lady was afraid to go to bed. She was standing on the banquette, confiding her alarms to some of her neighbors, when officer Boullosa, who had heard something of the matter, passed along. He inquired into the trouble, and was enlightened. He volunteered to enter the house and search it. Hailing two firemen, who happened to be passing, he got them to assist him in the search, and they entered the house. As they passed along the hall, a fly-brush was thrown at them by some one at the head of the stairs; and looking up quickly, the officer caught a glimpse of a retreating petticoat. They rushed up and gave chase, but the petticoat had disappeared. They searched the house thoroughly and found nobody. At last they noticed a door communicating to the adjoining house. This door was forced, and there, on the other side, they found the ghost—a very Ethiopian ghost, for whose arrest ten dollars reward was offered. She had been there secreted all the time, for no other purpose than to make noises in her mistress house at night, and to frighten her into the belief that the dead girl's ghost was after her.

Boullosa got his ten dollars, and the old lady got her nigger back and dropped her faith in ghosts. We did not hear whether or not the wench was treated to the flogging she so richly deserved.

HONOLULU, MAY 26, 1860.

Polynesian, Honolulu, Oahu, Hawaiian Islands, May 26, 1860, pg. 3.

TO THE EDITOR OF THE POLYNESIAN.
Appearance of a Ghost in Honolulu.

SIR:—It is well known that the celebrated (hobby) horse "Protection" has been dead a long time. The origin of this animal is somewhat obscure, but he is supposed to have been born in England. One Adam Smith, many years ago, having discovered that he was of a worthless breed, although very taking to the eye, patriotically gave him a blow from which he never recovered. A certain jockey, named Bobby Peel, who had a great fancy for the animal, tried a long time after, by careful nursing and stimulant's, to bring him round and present him again on the course, but finding at length that he was completely gone in the knees, he gave him a finishing blow and put him out of his misery.

Since that time (strange to relate) the ghost of this animal has every now and then appeared in different countries. We have had two appearances in the Sandwich Islands[38] within the last six or seven years, but after playing some antics, and like a Will-o'-the-wisp, leading a few misguided followers into quagmire and difficulties, the spectre on both occasions disappeared as mysteriously as it came.

It is now reported to have been seen again in Honolulu, having taken a very distinct and palpable shape. It should be immediately exorcised, as the native population (being taken with nothing so soon as a showy horse, however worthless,) might be led into danger. They should at once be instructed to be careful not to follow a phantom, and be warned of the risk of losing the substance by grasping at the shadows.

Port Tobacco Times and Charles County Advertiser, Port Tobacco, Maryland, July 26, 1860, pg. 1.

The man who wouldn't pay the printer is now haunted by the ghost of an editor's baby. So-says an exchange.

New-York Daily Tribune, New York, New York, July 27, 1860, pg. 5.

The old Van Winkles[39] and Knickerbockers[40] of Albany were dreadfully alarmed by the appearance, a few nights since, of a ghost in their midst. A building in course of construction and nearly finished was the place where the perturbed spirit performed its nocturnal peregrinations. It was a noisy ghost, and was heard but not seen. It was of the rapping and tumbling order, and created such a racket that the whole neighborhood for some distance

---

[38] Hawaii

[39] Rip Van Winkle was a character in Washington Irving's short story "Rip Van Winkle" published in 1819. The story is set in the Catskill Mountains.

[40] A Knickerbocker is a descendant of the early Dutch settlers of New York.

around was disturbed, and even the sluggish inhabitants of the old Dutch burgh were unable to sleep. They therefore left their beds, and to the number of two or three hundred surrounded the house, all at such distances from it, however, as would give them an advantageous start should his ghostship be disposed to sally forth to attack them.

"Ghost With A Revolver," Illustrated Police News, October 10, 1885

At length a police officer, who, for the simple reason that he had never seen a ghost, did not believe there was any such living (or dead) thing entered the building. The "honest old burghers" were astounded at his temerity, and stood, with mouths agape, in "breathless silence," awaiting the result. The officer soon reappeared, having captured the ghost, whom he held in a firm grasp upon his coat collar. It was soon ascertained that the cause of the fright was none other than a poor vagrant—a public character—who is kept for the policemen to practice or arrests upon, each one having a chance at him each day. The frightened citizens returned to their beds, to sleep an extra hour in the morning to make up for the one they had lost in ghost hunting.

Cincinnati Daily Press, Cincinnati, Ohio, August 2, 1860, pg. 1.

A GHOST ARRESTED BY POLICEMAN.—The Albany (N.Y.) *Knickerbocker* of late date, says that some excitement was created the other evening over strange noises that emanated from a house in course of construction, and now nearly finished. They could not be accounted for, although so loud and violent they could be heard two blocks off. They fell upon the ear of Officer Casper Langhor, who promptly went in search. On arriving at the spot he found a large crowd congregated. All seemed to be afraid to enter the place, being carried away with that foolish superstition of "haunted-house."

The officer screwed his courage up to its sticking point[41] and boldly entered. Soon after he had passed out of sight the noises could be heard vanishing, as though he had driven them out before him. All was now still. The crowd stood outside in breathless silence, to hear the result of the officer's adventure. Soon he made his appearance, having the ghost—a living one—by the collar. It was no less a personage than the redoubtable Francis Golden, city porter. Golden was marched to the station-house, and afterward received a sentence of ten days in the Penitentiary.

---

[41] "But screw your courage to the sticking place,/And we'll not fair," from William Shakespeare's play *Macbeth*, Act 1, scene 7, 59-61.

The Burlington Free Press.

Burlington Free Press, Burlington, Vermont,
August 17, 1860, pg. 1.

PERSONAL.

We have been informed by one who professed to know, and who was in a position to know, that Dr. Cogswell, of the Astor Library (now abroad for his health), lays at Mr. Bancroft's[42] door the promulgation of the absurd story about Dr. C.'s seeing a ghost in the Library, which had such a run through the papers, two or three months since,—and may be running still, for ought we know. The Doctor's statement, as repeated to us, is that he related to a circle of three or four, of whom Mr. Bancroft was one, the particulars of a striking dream which he had a night or two before. To his astonishment, in a day or two, his dream appeared, in the *Evening Post* if we remember aright, dressed up as a veritable ghost story.

Bellows Falls Times, Bellows Falls, Vermont,
August 24, 1860, pg. 1.

A person, pretending to have seen a ghost, was asked what the apparition said to him. "How should I know?" he replied; "I am not skilled in the dead languages!"

Daily Intelligencer, Wheeling, Virginia,
August 30, 1860, pg. 3.

---

[42] George Bancroft (1800-1891) was an American historian.

A SPOOK.—An Irish woman, living in the vicinity of the old jail, has several evenings lately seen and conversed with a very ghost, which came stalking into the house like the "goblin damned"[43] in the most questionable shape. Night before last, Colonius, the philosopher of the *Staats Zeitung*,[44] without the fear of slung shots and loafers, much less of Spooks, before his eyes, went up in company with others to watch for his ghostship. He gives an item about it, but testifies that, although he watched long and wearily, he saw no ghost. He thinks the whole thing had its origin in whiskey and recommends lager beer.

Chicago Daily Tribune, Chicago, Illinois, October 29, 1860, pg. 2.

The Ghost of Barracks Street, New Orleans—A Horrible Discovery.

For some three weeks past there has been considerable excitement among the negroes who live in the neighborhood of Barracks street, New Orleans, in consequence of a report that the ghost of a free-colored man, who blew out his brains in that locality, was in the habit of occasionally emerging from his late residence and indulging in his midnight strolls, clad in vestments of the most unearthly whiteness. Many negroes saw the ghost, and some had even approached it, in which case they saw it always sank slowly into the earth. This story at length spread among white people, and there were not a few who had satisfied their curiosity by midnight visits to the locality and were ready to take oath that the ghost story was no fabrication. At length it even obtained credit with the police, and two night watchmen got their beats removed to other streets from this one. One of these declared the ghost to be over ten feet high, and of ghostly visage. This had to be investigated, as there could be no doubt but that there was

---

[43] "Be thou a spirit of health of goblin damned…"from William Shakespeare's play *Hamlet*, Act 1, scene 4, 43.

[44] *Virginische Staats-Zeitung* a German newspaper published in Wheeling, Virginia from 1848 to 1863. In 1860 the paper was edited by Henry Colonius.

some ground for their stories, which attracted numbers of people on foot and in cabs, every midnight to Barracks street, one of those matter-of-fact men in whose minds the supernatural element finds little room. He walked up to the ghost the other night, and catching firm hold of it, discovered it be a poor old half crazy woman who wonders out of her house at this time with her white undershirts drawn up over her head. The mystery was fathomed, and the locality has now lost all its former interest.—*New Orleans Bee*.

Daily Dispatch, Richmond, Virginia, November 7, 1860, pg. 1.

Singular Case.—On Saturday night, a young lady residing on Church Hill was retiring to her apartment, and on reaching the top of the steps, encountered what is termed an "apparition"—in other words, thought she saw a ghost. Her fright found utterance in a fearful shriek, which attracted the attention of her friends, who hastened to the spot and discovered her in a swoon. She was restored to consciousness with great difficulty, and has not fully recovered from the shock. The circumstance shows to what an extent the imagination may influence the mind.

Evening Star, Washington, D.C., November 7, 1860, pg. 1.

MINOT'S LEDGE LIGHT-HOUSE[45]—The interior of this structure is being rapidly completed. The workmen labor on it night and day. The woodwork of the house, we believe, is entirely of oak, and will be when finished, as solid and enduring as it can be made. Workmen at work in the night report that during the severest storms thus far only a slight trembling is felt. Capt. Alexander, who superintended the construction of the light house,

---

[45] Minot's Ledge Lighthouse is located one mile offshore of the towns of Cohasset and Scituate, Massachusetts.

dined within its granite walls, one day last week, with his entire family. Report says that one man who recently spent a night in the building could not be induced to try the experiment again. Airy phantoms disturbed his quiet—visions, apparitions, fantastic shapes flitted around him, and among the rest, the veritable ghosts of the two brave but unfortunate men who perished when the iron light house yielded to the stormy waves.[46] Now, those men, it is true, went down alive into the remorseless deep, with none to tell the dismal story of their end; but as for their ghosts coming back and haunting the new structure to terrify and torment their successors, we don't believe one single word of it. It is a libel on the dead. The sympathizing ghosts of those men, full of pity and compassion for their successors, would be the very last ghosts in the universe to haunt the brave men who should fearlessly step into their shoes.—*Hingham Journal.*

Minot's Ledge Lighthouse in a 2010 storm.

[46] The original Minot's Ledge Lighthouse was destroyed in a storm in April 1851. Fishermen still report hearing the sounds of crying coming from the lighthouse from the ghosts of the lighthouse keepers who perished in 1851. For more about the legends of Minot's Ledge Lighthouse see http://www.newenglandhistoricalsociety.com/minots-ledge-light-dangerous-romantic-lighthouse-america/ (accessed August 11, 2018).

Cincinnati Daily Press, Cincinnati, Ohio,
November 10, 1860, pg. 1.

APPEARANCE OF GHOSTS ON A RAILWAY.—The Burlington (Iowa) *Hawkeye* is responsible for the following:

The queer sights at night on the Chicago and Burlington Railroad still continue. An engineer on the road says that as he was approaching Galesburg, a few nights since, he suddenly saw a woman standing upon the track about ten feet ahead of the engine. The train was at full speed, and, of course, could not be stopped. The engineer remarked to the persons on the engine that that was the first person he had ever killed during his railroad experience. Arriving at the depot, he sent men and lights back to the spot where he saw the woman, but no sign or trace of any thing was there. There was no body, no blood, no marks upon the track. Next morning the search was renewed, but no better success. It is said that lights have been seen, lighting several acres of land with the brilliancy of noon-day.[47]

THE WEEKLY LANCASTER GAZETTE.

THE UNION OF THE STATES—ONE COUNTRY—ONE DESTINY.

VOL. 1.   LANCASTER, OHIO, THURSDAY, NOV. 29, 1860.   NO. 35.

The Weekly Lancaster Gazette, Lancaster, Ohio,
November 29, 1860, pg. 3.

GHOSTS.—There are strange stories afloat concerning these dwellers in the nether world. Our friend "John" and "Sam" saw one of these mysterious creatures a few night since, and no mistake. It was tall and spare-dressed in a shroud and was seen in the inevitable grave yard.

Our friends, forgetting the stories of the "lame goose," and the innocent "signpost," were frightened out of their wits. John's teeth chattered and Sam's hair raised up until it not only raised his hat off his head, but actually lifted him out of his boots. The ghost

---

[47] This phenomenon is also known as Spook Lights.

suddenly vanished and so did our friends. The story was told. The credulous old woman, and *some* young women are terribly alarmed. They see ghosts in every corner and their dreams are full of them.

New Orleans Daily Crescent, New Orleans, Louisiana, December 3, 1860, pg. 3.

The Ghost in the Tower.

We find in "Notes and Queries" the following ghost story, which is related by Edmund Lenthal Swifte:[48]

I have often purposed to leave behind me a faithful record of all that I personally know of this strange story. Forty-three years have passed, and its impression is as vividly before me as on the moment of its occurrence. Ancedotage, said Wilkes,[49] is an old man's dotage; and at 83 I may be suspected of lapsing into omissions or exaggerations; but there are yet survivors who can testify that I have not at any time either amplified or abridged my ghostly experience.

In 1814, I was appointed keeper of the crown jewels in the Tower, where I resided with my family till my retirement in 1852. One Saturday night in October, 1817, about "the witching hour," I was at supper with my wife, our little boy, and her sister, in the sitting-room of the Jewel House, which, then comparatively modernized, is said to have been the "doleful prison" of Anna Boleyn,[50] and one of the ten bishops whom Oliver Cromwell[51] piously accommodated therein. The room was, and still is, irregularly shaped, having three doors and two windows, which last are out nearly nine feet deep into the outer wall; between these

---

[48] Edmund Lenthal Swifte (1777-1875) was an English writer, poet, lawyer and custodian of the British Crown Jewels at the Tower of London.

[49] John Wilkes (1727-1797) was an English journalist and politician.

[50] Queen Anne Boleyn (c. 1501-1536) was the notorious second wife of King Henry VIII; she was executed at the Tower of London for adultery. Legend holds that Anne Boleyn's ghost haunts the Tower of London.

[51] Oliver Cromwell (1599-1658), the Lord Protector of the Commonwealth of England, Scotland, and Ireland from 1653-1658.

is a chimney-piece projecting far into the room, and (then) surmounted with a large oil picture. On the night in question the doors were all closed, heavy and dark cloth curtains were let down over the windows, and the only light in the room was that of two candles on the table.

I sat at the foot of the table, my son on my right hand, his mother fronting the chimney-piece, and her sister on the opposite side. I had offered a glass of wine-and-water, when, on putting it to her lips, she paused, and exclaimed, "Good God! what is that?" I looked up, and saw a cylindrical figure, like a glass tube, seemingly about the thickness of my arm, and hovering between the ceiling and table; its contents appeared to be a dense fluid, white and pale azure, like to the gathering of a summer cloud and incessantly rolling and mingling within the cylinder. This lasted about two minutes, when it began slowly to move before my sister-in-law; then, following the oblong shape of the table, before my son and myself; passing behind my wife, it paused for a moment over her right shoulder. Observe, there was no mirror opposite to her in which she could behold it. Instantly she crouched down, and, with both hands covering her shoulder, she shrieked out, "Oh, Christ? it has seized me!" Even now, while writing, I feel the fresh horror of that moment. I caught up my chair, struck at the wainscot behind her, rushed up stairs to the other children's room, and told the terrified nurse what I had seen. Meanwhile, the other domestics had hurried into the parlor, where their mistress recounted to them the scene, even as I was detailing it above stairs.

The marvel—some will say absurdity—of all this is enhanced by the fact that neither my sister-in-law nor my son beheld this "appearance."

Following hard at heel the visitation of my household, one of the night sentries at the Jewel Office was, as he said, alarmed by a figure like a huge bear[52] issuing from underneath the door: he thrust at it with his bayonet, which struck in the door, even as my chair dinted the wainscot; he dropped into a fit, and was carried senseless to the guard-room. His fellow-sentry declared that the man was neither asleep nor drunk, he himself having seen him a

---

[52] Wild animals were kept in the Royal Menagerie in the Tower of London from c. 1210-1830.

moment before awoke and sober. Of all this, I avouch nothing more than I saw the poor man in the guardhouse, prostrated with terror, and that in two or three days the "fatal result," be it of fact or fancy, was—*that he died.*[53]

My story may claim more sparse than you can afford: desiring to be circumstantial, I have been diffuse. This I leave to the editor's discretion: let it only be understood that to all which I have therein set forth as seen by myself, I absolutely pledge my faith and my honor.

STAUNTON, VIRGINIA, TUESDAY, DECEMBER 4, 1860.

Staunton Spectator, Staunton, Virginia, December 4, 1860, pg. 1.

The Dead Child's Ghost.

The New York Presbyterian of a late date relates this story:

We were returning from our Spring meeting of Presbytery—one gentleman and two young ladies—in a "rockaway,"[54] and the road none of the best. Night, cold and damp, overtook us eight or ten miles from home, but only a short distance from Judge Blank's, who, after we had arrived at his house, narrated the following unique tale. Said the Judge as follows:

"Years ago we had in our house a sweet little child, about four years of age, and the object, of course, of a very tender affection. But sickness laid its hand upon it. Remedies, promptly resorted to, all proved in vain. Day after day the rose faded from the cheek, and the fire in the eyes burned low; and at length death

---

[53] This event occurred in January 1816, a year before Swifte's sighting in October 1817.

[54] A rockaway is a type of carriage popular in the 19th-century.

closed those eyes and sealed those lips forever; and we learned by trying experience how intense darkness follows the quenching of one of those little lights of life.

"The time rolling sadly on, brought us at length to the hour appointed for committing our treasure to the ordinary custody of the grave.—The friends assembled, the customary services were held, the farewell taken, and the little form securely shut beneath the well-screwed coffin-lid, and in due form the grave received its trust. We looked on and saw the earth thrown in, the mound raised above, and the plates of sod neatly adjusted into a great sheltering roof.—We then wended our way back to our desolate home. Evening came on and wore away. My wife had gone into an adjoining room to give some directions to a servant, and I, unfitted by the scene of the day for aught else, had just laid my head on my pillow in our room upon the first floor of the house, when I heard a shriek, and in a moment more my wife came flying into the room, and springing upon the bed behind me, exclaimed—

"See there! our child! our child!

"Raising my head, my blood froze within me, and the hair upon my head stood up, as I saw the little thing in grave clothes, with open, but manifestly sightless eyes, and pale as when we gave it the last kiss, walking slowly towards us. Had I been alone—had not the extreme terror of my wife compelled me to play the man, I should have leaped from the window and bed without casting a look behind.

"But, not daring to leave her in such terror, I arose, sat down in a chair, and took the little creature between my knees—a cold sweat covered my body—and gazed with feelings unutterable upon the object before me. The eyes were open in vacant stare.

MISCELLANY.

The Dead Child's Ghost.

The New York Presbyterian of a late date relates this story:

We were returning from our Spring meeting of Presbytery—one gentleman and two young ladies—in a "rockaway," and the road none of the best. Night, cold and damp, overtook us eight or ten miles from home, but only a short distance from Judge Blank's, who, after we had arrived at his house, narrated the following unique tale. Said the Judge as follows:

"Years ago we had in our house a sweet little child, about four years of age, and the object, of course, of a very tender affection. But sickness laid its hand upon it. Remedies, promptly resorted to, all proved in vain. Day after day the rose faded from the cheek, and the fire in the eyes burned low; and at length death closed those eyes and sealed those lips forever; and we learned by trying experience how intense darkness follows the quenching of one of those little lights of life.

The flesh was colorless, cold and clammy; nor did the child appear to have the power of either speech or hearing, as it made no attempt to answer any of our questions. The horror of our minds was the more intense as we had watched our child through its sickness and death, and had been but a few hours before eye-witness if its interment.

"While gazing upon it, and asking in my silent thoughts, 'what can this extraordinary providence mean? for what can it be sent?' the servant girl, having crept to the door, after a time, suggested, it looks like Mrs.—'s child.

"Now our neighbor had a child about the same age as ours, and its constant companion.—But what could bring it to our home at that hour and in such a plight? Still the suggestion had operated as a sedative upon our excited feelings, and rendered us more capable of calm reflection. And, after a time, we discovered in truth, that the *grave* clothes were *night* clothes, and the corpse a somnambulist.[55] And it became manifest that the excitement attending the loss and burial of its playmate working upon the child's mind in sleep, was the cause to which we were indebted from this untimely and startling visit.

"Wiping away the perspiration and taking a few long breaths, I prepared to countermarch the little intruder back to its forsaken bed.—Back we went, it keeping at my side, though still asleep. It had walked quite a distance across the wet grass. I found the door of its home ajar, just as the fugitive had left it, and its sleeping parents unconscious of its absence.—The door creaked as I pushed it open, and the noise awakened the child, who looked wildly around a moment, and then popped into bed.

"Now, if it had not been for my wife, as I have said, I should, on the appearance of this apparition, have made a leap of uncommon agility from that window; and after a flight of uncommon velocity for a person of my age and dignity, I should have been ready to take an oath in any court, either in Christendom or heathendom, that I had seen a ghost."

---

[55] Sleepwalker

Michelle Hamilton

1861

Cleveland Morning Leader, Cleveland, Ohio, January 30, 1861, pg. 1.

SPIRITUAL INTELLIGENCE.—That ghost, or if not that ghost, another ghost, still continues his moon-light flitting. He may now be seen for a few night only, on or about Prospect street. It was on this street, a night or two since, that a merry young gentleman, accompanied by two lovely ladies, was wending his reluctant way homeward from a party, which he had attended in the neighborhood, when in the midst of a lively and interesting conversation, an unearthly, and hideous groan was heard, proceeding directly behind them. The young man is by no means a person to be frightened by ordinary events; but to be attacked by an incarnate creature, in this off hand and familiar sort of style; to be morally squared off at, by an object which it is an utter impossibility to "punch," or in otherwise, to maltreat; that is altogether an other thing. It is no wonder therefore that his voice was slightly tremulous, when sustaining his fainting companions, he inquired his ghostship's pleasure. A repetition of the groan was the only audible reply, but a shadowy arm was extended, and a skeleton finger beckoned him closer.

This was too much. It was imposing on good nature; it was taking advantage of fortuitous circumstances; and so the merry young man, and the two lovely young ladies did, what probably most of us would have done sooner: they looked—they turned—

they fled. The ghost did not pursue; it is seldom indeed that they do, and therefore nothing serious resulted, but it is probable that a certain young man, whenever he has occasion after this, to return home about the hour of midnight, will take some other avenue beside Prospect street.

THE BRADFORD REPORTER.

PUBLISHED EVERY THURSDAY AT TOWANDA, BRADFORD COUNTY, PA., BY R. W. STURROCK.

VOL. XXI.—NO. 35

Bradford Reporter, Towanda, Pennsylvania, January 31, 1861, pg. 1.

A GHOST—One of our devils says he saw a ghost—it was white, flew up over a fence, looked like a white woman, a white dog, or goose, or something else; thinks it might probably have been something else, but is positive it was a ghost, as he saw it himself—though he don't believe in such trash. That boy stays off the streets after dark just about this time.

The Lancaster Ledger, Lancaster, South Carolina, February 6, 1861, pg. 1.

A Ghost Story.

The following is from the San Francisco Alta Californian:

Several weeks ago a married lady residing in the Sandwich Islands, who had come to this city for her health, and was boarding at a house on California street, woke in the night and plainly saw a phantom of her husband, and in that supposition, called to her son, a boy of about twelve years of age, saying: "Henry, here's your father." She got up, and advanced towards the figure and it disappeared. She pinched herself, to see whether she was not asleep, but found herself to be fully awake. The vision disturbed her very much; notwithstanding the fact that she had left her husband in good health at Honolulu, a few weeks before, she feared greatly that the vision indicated his death. When she went down to breakfast in the morning, a gentleman boarding in the same house noticed the mark of weeping, and endeavored to get her into a good humor. She told him the cause of her uneasiness, and attempted to remove the unhappy impression from her mind, but failed. She insisted that her husband must be dead, and that she must return to Honolulu by the first boat, and so she did. A few days after her departure a vessel arrived from Honolulu with news that her husband had died. His death, however, did not take place on the day when she saw the vision, but a week before.

Cincinnati Daily Press, Cincinnati, Ohio,
February 9, 1861, pg. 3.

TRUTHFUL REVELATIONS OF A GHOST IN ENGLAND.—The *European Times*, of Liverpool, says:

A curious affair is reported from Kendal. A young woman, who had been ill some time, stated the other day that a ghost had come to her while she lay in bed, and spoke in a thick, husky, hollow voice, telling her, while pointing in the direction below, to follow him to the cellar of the house, where, on removing the flagstone on the hearth, something would be found buried, which was the special purpose of his visit to reveal. On stating this, the form of the unearthly visitant vanished like a dim shadow.

Slowly and silently the parties in the house went to the locality in the cellar pointed out by the man in black—dug up the hearth-flag, and found a quantity of bones (which yet remain for the inspection of the curious) buried a little below the surface. A quantity of hops, in good preservation, were found scattered here and there over the soil. These bones (human they are said to be by some accounted competent judges in such matters) have been examined by scores of people. Their state of decay leads to the supposition that a long, long time had elapsed since they were put beneath the ground.

Cincinnati Daily Press.

VOL: IV, NO. 172.　　　CINCINNATI, MONDAY MORNING, FEBRUARY 11, 1861.　　　PRICE ONE CENT

Cincinnati Daily Press, Cincinnati, Ohio,
February 11, 1861, pg. 1.

A GHOST STORY AND DISCOVERY OF A MYSTERIOUS CRIME.— The Alexandria (Va.) *Gazette* has the particulars of a curious ghost story. The people living in the house of No. 11 Wolf-street had long been annoyed by "mysterious knockings," and had concluded that the house was haunted. One man, having heard that old Mrs. Rye had died in the house about a year ago, thought that perhaps she had hid some treasure during her life, and that her spirit was uneasy about it, and wanted some one to find it.

So he thought he might as well as not be that some one, and went to work on Saturday morning. He made a search, and found in one of the cuddy holes between the rafters, under the eaves of the house, the sewed-up leg of a pair of black pantaloons, upon seeing which an indescribable sensation pervaded his whole frame, and he hastily retreated from the place. He thought he had a fortune sure, and went to get a neighbor to witness him taking possession.

The neighbor came, the pantaloons leg was pulled out, also an old coat, sewed up into a bundle. The package were carefully opened, and found to contain—not a parcel of coin and bills, but two dead bodies, carefully packed in lime. A copy of the

Charlestown *Free Press*, of February, 1860, was also brought to light, showing that the horrid murder of these two little innocents must have taken place a year ago at least. There was a "crowner's quest,"[56] when the following verdict was returned by the jury:

"That they are unable to find when, how, and by what means the infants came to their death; but, from the circumstances, they believe that death was feloniously caused by some person or persons unknown."

The Daily Exchange, Baltimore, Maryland, February 16, 1861, pg. 1.

AN OLD FASHIONED GHOST STORY.
THE GHOST REVEALS A MURDER.

A late number of the Kendal (England) *Mercury* tells this story:

"There is a cottage at the upper end of Kitty Gibson's yard, which is occupied by a man named Joseph Allinson. One of the inmates, a young woman named Marian Allan, sister of Mrs. Allinson, who has been bedridden and nearly blind for some time past, is the "medium" through which the strange story now in circulation has been set afloat. It appears that on Monday evening last, whilst some five or six men and women were sitting by the fireside down stairs, all at once they were alarmed by some heavy sounds, as if some one was knocking violently in a room upstairs; this noise continued for some time—knock—knock—knock— louder and louder—so much so that the concussion shook the house as if it were about to be brought down altogether—one person stating that the chair in which he was sitting was fairly lifted up. On their proceeding to her apartment the young woman gave forth this curious revelation: An apparition had visited her (which she was permitted to behold for a time, and then her eyesight left her as before), the figure of a man dressed in black, of a grim and rough aspect. She describes something breathed in her

---

[56] Coroner's inquest

face—that 'the lighted candle in the room burned dim, and finally, either went out of its own accord or was extinguished by some unseen hand, when the figure appeared as stated.—On acquiring sufficient utterance, she inquired of the ghost, in the name of the Holy Trinity, why she was troubled with his presence. On the third time of asking, the spectre spoke in a thick, husky hollow voice, telling her, whilst pointing in the direction below, to follow him to the cellar of the house, where, on removing the flagstone on the hearth, something would be found buried, which, it was the special purpose of his visit to reveal….

Cleveland Morning Leader, Cleveland, Ohio, March 20, 1861, pg. 1.

THAT GHOST AGAIN.—The ghost which was wont to promenade Erie and Prospect streets, has become emboldened by the impunity with which it has walked, and two or three nights since appeared upon Seneca street, between St. Clair and Lake, terribly frightening some children who were going home from a visit. This style of practical joking has gone too far and must be stopped. Some nervous person may yet be so frightened by the reckless person who personates a ghost, as to cause serious injury and perhaps death. Any man, young or old, who will indulge in such performances, is a public nuisance and should be abated in the most expedient and effectual manner. His person should be no more respected than that of a burglar or highway robber.

Cleveland Morning Leader, Cleveland, Ohio, March 22, 1861, pg. 1.

GETTING TO BE A NUISANCE.—It is our business to deal with temporal rather than with spiritual things, but when such an unconscionable ill-bred "ghost" exists in our midst as the one which perambulates the streets almost every night, going to and fro unmolested, and frightening men, women and children out of their senses, we feel bound to protect against it. Hamlet's father[57] was a fool to this shade. On Tuesday night he was seen again on Wednesday night, both on Seneca and Chestnut streets which shows that his range is a wide one. Certainly, the police ought to take the matter and the ghost too, in hand.

Cleveland Morning Leader.

R. Cowles & Co., Publishers,   Office No. 144 Superior Street.   Terms, $3 ...

VOL. XV.   CLEVELAND, SATURDAY MORNING, MARCH 23, 1861   NO. 69.

Cleveland Morning Leader, Cleveland, Ohio, March 23, 1861, pg. 1.

THE GHOST.—We have heard of at least three cases of nervous debility, caused by meeting the follow who has recently been playing the part of a ghost about the streets. On Thursday night there were probably from seventy-five to one hundred persons on the watch, but we have not heard that any of them met with the object of their curiosity.

Cleveland Morning Leader, Cleveland, Ohio, March 27, 1861, pg. 1.

MORE ABOUT THE GHOST.—A few more stories about 'the ghost' and we shall begin to believe that he is actually an unquiet spirit, doomed to wander his allotted season on this side the Styx.[58] Tales are told which, if they are to be believed—and who doubt them?—would place the matter

---

[57] King Hamlet's ghost appears to his son at the start of William Shakespeare's play *Hamlet*.

[58] In ancient Greek mythology Styx is both the god of the dead and the name for the river that served as a boundary to the underworld.

beyond question.—One young lady informs us that the apparition has been seen to glide noiselessly along the ground until near the cemetery gates, when it rose gradually into the air and disappeared from the sight of the amazed beholder. Another has seen the spectral form on a coal-black steed galloping madly along the road at dead of night. If all the marvelous accounts that have come to our ears, were collected and printed, it is to be doubted if anything less in size than a "blanket sheet" would contain them. Among the practical jokes incident to the appearance of the Phenomenon, was one played upon a worthy officer in the police force who had been spending rather a jolly evening with some lady friends.

At leaving he was dismissed through a side door, and from thence walked around to the front gate where he beheld a tall figure standing with extended arms and clad in the pale garments of an unearthly visitor. But this officer has too much good muscle to be "a feared" of a being which is so deficient in that respect, and before a watch could tick once, his hand had grasped something very like ordinary flesh and blood, and the figure was on the way to the Station House. A loud scream, however, soon testified to two facts; one, that it wasn't *the* ghost, another that it was of the number of those with whom, a moment previously he had been innocently sporting. How the matter was compromised we are unable to state.

Fayetteville Observer, Fayetteville, North Carolina, March 28, 1861, pg. 1.

A Supernatural Phenomenon—Story of a Railroad Engineer.—I was running a night express train, with ten cars—eight passenger and two baggage cars—and all were well loaded. I was behind time, and was very anxious to make a certain point, thus I was using every exertion, and putting the engine to the utmost speed to which she was capable. I was on a section of the road usually considered the best running ground on the line, and was endeavoring to make the most of it, when a conviction struck me that I must stop.

A something seemed to tell me that to go ahead was dangerous, and that I must stop if I would save life. I looked back at my train, and it was all right. I strained my eyes and peered into the darkness, and could see no signal of danger nor anything betokening danger, and there I could see five miles in daytime. I listened to the working of my engine, tried the water, looked at the gauge, and all was right. I tried to laugh myself out of what I then considered a childish fear; but, like Banquo's[59] ghost, it would not down my bidding, but grew stronger in its hold upon me.

I thought of the ridicule I would have heaped upon me if I did stop; but it was all of no avail. The conviction—for by this time it had ripened into a conviction—that I must stop grew stronger, and I shut off and blew the whistle for breakers accordingly. I came to a dead halt, got off, and went ahead a little way, without saying anything to any body what the matter was. I had a lamp in my hand, and had gone about sixty feet, when I saw what convinced me that premonitions are sometimes possible. I dropped the lantern from my nerveless grasp, and set down on the track utterly unable to stand, for there was a switch, the thought of which had never been used since I had been on the road, and was known to be spiked, but was open to lead me off the track. This switch led into a stone quarry, from whence stone for bridge purposes had been quarried, and the switch was left there is case stone should be needed at any time, but it was always locked, and the switch rail spiked.

Yet here it was wide open, and had I not obeyed my premonition—warning—call it what you will—I should have run into it, and, at the end of the track, only about ten rods long, my heavy engine and train, moving at the rate of thirty miles per hour, would have come into collision with a solid wall of rock, eighteen feet high. The consequences, had I done so, can neither be imagined nor described; but they could, by no possibility, have been otherwise than fatally horrid. This is my experience in getting warnings from a source that I know not, and can not divine. It is a mystery to me—a mystery for which I am very thankful,

---

[59] Banquo appeared as a ghost following his murder in William Shakespeare's play *Macbeth*.

however, although I dare not attempt to explain nor say whence it came.

The Hancock Jeffersonian, Findlay, Ohio, March 29, 1861, pg. 2.

Current News.

They are having a terrible time over a ghost, in Cleveland, which has been playing off its fantastic tricks, to the no small annoyance of the credulous. Great efforts have been made to capture it, but thus far, it has managed to slip through their fingers. It is seen sometimes riding, sometimes walking, and sometimes flying, but won't "down," with all the power of incantation brought to bear it.

Cincinnati Daily Press, Cincinnati, Ohio, March 29, 1861, pg. 1.

A little girl was badly frightened in Cleveland, Ohio, a few days ago, by seeing a "ghost," and has since died.

Cleveland Morning Leader, Cleveland, Ohio, March 29, 1861, pg. 1.

IDLE GHOST STORIES.—Of the infinite number of stories told about the ghost which has perambulated our streets, only about one in a hundred is entitled to the least credit.—The others are all gotten up for effect. It is so pleasant to be looked upon as a hero, and so easy to manufacture that reputation by asserting that you saw and chased the ghost until it vanished, that the temptation is often too strong to be resisted.

Among the flying rumors has been one that Miss Wrightman, daughter of D. L. Wrightman, Esq., was so badly frightened as to be seriously injured by a sight of the spiritual visitant. We are requested by Mr. Wrightman's family to state that the whole story is a sheer fabrication, and that the young lady first heard of the terrible fright from outside friends.

Nine-tenths of all the ghost stories, if traced to their source, would be found equally deficient in fact.

President Lincoln in Cleveland, OH, *Frank Leslie's Illustrated Newspaper*, Mar. 2, 1861.

Ashtabula Weekly Telegraph, Ashtabula, Ohio, March 30, 1861, pg. 3.

GHOSTS.—The people of Cleveland are troubled with goblins that stalk their streets at night, causing a deal of apprehension. His ghostship is sometimes seen a-foot, and sometimes a-horesback, sometimes he is seen at a distance in giant proportions, at others in narrow allies and lowly sheds and shanties. Great vigilance is put into requisition to capture the "ghost of goblin damned," but hitherto without success. He was run into a shed the other night and surrounded, but when the shed was entered to capture him, no one was found but a very much frightened stranger, who had witnessed his entry but could give no account of his disappearance, and as there was no regalia, such as ghosts wear, visible, the conclusion seems to have been arrived at that the creature had evaporated in thin air. Had the thing been seen about the office of the *Plain Dealer*, there could have been very little conjecture as to its object, for if the devil does not get hold of GRAY soon, the design of such an institution as a devil will seem to be frustrated.

Cleveland Morning Leader, Cleveland, Ohio, March 30, 1861, pg. 2.

THE GHOST HUNTERS.

We have a ghost in Cleveland,
And every night you'll meet
A score or more of hunters bold
Patrolling every street.

Down every lane and doorway,
Through church yard and through square;
There's not a street in the city at night,
But some ghost hunters are there.

Near the sty[60] of sleepin' porkers,
Through the cemetery dismal and damp,
On the shore of beautiful Erie,
You can hear the ghost hunters tramp.

You can hear their shout through the stilly night,
And the noise of their measured tread
Would scare away any peaceable ghost,
Or awaken the sleep of the dead.

Some are armed with pitch forks,
And some with guns and sword,
And a captain bold with a pair of shears
From off his tailors board

---

[60] A pigsty

But vain are their efforts to catch him,
They have frightened his ghost-ship away,
And back he has gone with his winding sheet on,
To his grave in the cold, cold day.

There let him remain forever,
Let no one disturb his repose,
For he has promised to send us a letter,
And the secrets of his wandering disclose.

When we get it we'll surely print it;
Meanwhile our customers all
Are invited to call and see the spring stock
At ISAACS' UNION HALL.

Daily Morning News, Savannah, Georgia,
March 30, 1861, pg. 2.

FRIGHTHNED AWAY BY GHOSTS.—The Crown Point (Ind.) Register is responsible for the following, the last ghost story:

A little south of Crown Point, probably two miles stands a house that is to some a wonder. The house of itself is nothing more than a building, say eighteen by twenty-four feet, and a story and a half high. Not many months since, a mother and daughter who occupied the house were taken sick, and in a few days died. There was nothing peculiar about their death, as any one observed. They were soon buried, and the house left vacant. Soon after a family moved in, and since then it has been occupied most of the time until within a few weeks, when it was found impossible for a family to reside there. For weeks they have seen manifestations of a supernatural presence. Besides the moving of all moveable articles, the tinking of glasses and the rattle of tinware, there were frequent and startling sounds, as of whispered conversations, singing, subdued laughter, all imitations of the human voice. These ghost have been seen at all hours of the night. An old lady, clad in her grave clothes, has been seen to come from the adjacent forest where the wind swept in tremendous gusts, rattling the ley branches of the trees. She invariably walks around the house and sings a doleful tune, until she is joined by a young female, when the two unite in a plaintive song. Unusually, light footsteps are heard in the house, and at times the ghostly visitors are seen promenading [in] the kitchen and the other rooms of the house until a late hour of the night, and in some instances have not left till day-light. The family became so alarmed and troubled at these manifestations that they picked up their duds and left...the premises. We understand that no earthly consideration could induce them to remain.

Evening Star, Washington, D.C.,
April 1, 1861, pg. 1.

AN ITINERANT GHOST.—The prevailing sensation at Cleveland is a phantom of variable form and size which occasionally perambulates the streets of that city, after "the witching hour of night," to the intense terror of some score or more of timid persons who have enjoyed a glimpse of his ghostship, and the indignation of a still greater number who irreverently regard the nocturnal visitant as a miscreant worthy only of summary punishment. The latest doings of the apparition are thus related by the Cleveland Herald of Saturday:

So much indignation has been excited by his reported doings that on Tuesday night about one hundred and fifty persons were on watch for him. Many of the watchers were armed with pistols, and from at least some of them the ghost would have met a warm reception. No one prepared for an encounter has yet been so fortunate as to obtain a sight of the whitesheeted individual.

On Tuesday evening a young man, clerk in a Superior-st. store, was walking up Erie street, when he suddenly beheld the ghost a few feet to his right. The figure, he says, was 10 feet in height, and moved smoothly and noiselessly along. The young man remembers nothing more until he found himself lying on the ground, the ghost nowhere to be seen. He had fainted.

In the same neighborhood two boys encountered the pretended apparition a few nights since. Picking up a heavy stone,

one of the boys followed the figure, which was retreating towards an alley. Just as the ghost turned into the alley, the boy threw his stone, and with such correct aim that it struck the figure full in the back. A groan, unearthly enough, but too vigorous for any but sound lungs of flesh and blood, was the response.

Perhaps the ghost was admonished by this adventure that his nocturnal perambulations might be attended occasionally by disagreeable circumstances. Certain it is that when a man encountered it the next night, and proceeded to administer the castigation it so richly deserves, the ghost produced a most substantial cudgel,[61] with which he dealt his chastiser a blow that sent him reeling to the ground.

There are various accounts of the appearance of the figure. Some assert that when first seen it is no larger than an ordinary man, but immediately expands or enlarges to double that size. There is no "joke" in frightening people as this miscreant has done, and the person who catches and punishes the fellow will deserve the thanks of the community.

THE RED WING SENTINEL.

Minnesota Forever.

VOLUME 5, NUMBER 36.   WHOLE NUMBER 244.

RED WING, GOODHUE COUNTY, MINN., WEDNESDAY, APRIL 3, 1861.

Red Wing Sentinel, Red Wing, Minnesota, April 3, 1861, pg. 1.

GHOSTS AROUND.—The Buffalo Republican has got a sensation item in the shape of a ghost, as witness the following:

It is said that apparitions have been seen wandering about the premises of the late Clarendon hotel, in this city. Persons who have seen these nightly visitors describe them as having the appearance of two females, with candles in their hands, bent over and groping around, as if in search of something they had lost.

---

[61] A short thick stick used as a weapon.

They generally make their appearance at high twelve, the time when all ghosts are wont to "revisit the glimpse of the moon."[62] Certain it is that something like ghosts have been seen stalking in that vicinity; whether their intents be charitable or wicked has not leaked out. We are told the watchman on his midnight round has frequently came in sight of these nightly visitants, but as yet no sound or voice has been vouchsafed to mortal ears. What does it mean?

Holmes County Republican.

J. CINKEY, Editor and Proprietor.　　　OFFICE—Washington Street, Third Door South of Jackson.　　　TERMS—One Dollar and Fifty Cents in Advance

VOL. 5.　　　MILLERSBURG, HOLMES COUNTY, OHIO, THURSDAY, APRIL 4, 1861.　　　NO. 33

Holmes County Republican, Millersburg, Ohio, April 4, 1861, pg. 2.

The Clevelanders are getting a good deal excited about a certain ghost which it is said has been seen by sundry individuals in various parts of the city. Regularly organized parties are nightly on the look-out for the mysterious visitor.

> The Clevelanders are getting a good deal excited about a certain ghost which it is said has been seen by sundry individuals in various parts of the city. Regularly organized parties are nightly on the look-out for the mysterious visitor.

The Jeffersonian Democrat, Chardon, Ohio, April 5, 1861, pg. 2.

The Ghost—Who is it?

---

[62] "Revisits thus the glimpses of the moon," from William Shakespeare's play *Hamlet*, Act 1, Scene 4, 56.

Civil War Ghosts

That some scoundrel is prowling the streets almost nightly, disguising himself as the occasion and the person he meets give warrant, in ghostly garb, has now become a fixed fact, and the public mind is becoming greatly exercised upon the subject. Various parties of gentlemen have been out in pursuit of the miscreant, and though using every precaution, have as yet been unable to find and apprehend him. That there are many idle rumors in connection with this affair, it is unnecessary to say, but we have the testimony of the following persons, who are reliable, for the actual witnessing of this ghostly imposter.

Charles Gordon, son of Wm. J. Gordon, Esq., returning home one evening last week, met him in front of Dean's Store Block, on Water street.

James Armstrong, clerk at Davis, Peixotto & Co.'s met him last Wednesday night at quarter to twelve o'clock, in front of the Cathedral, Erin St. On picking up a brick to throw at him, the "Spectre" made off.

Dr. Beckwith, riding in his buggy, encountered him a few nights since.

John Hunter, clerk for F.C. Keith, going home at eleven o'clock Sunday night, passed him on Rackwell street near the corner of Erie.

A son of Mrs. John Gill encountered him on Erie street, near the Cemetery. On pointing a pistol at him, the cap of which failed to go off, the Ghost gave chase, and young Gill took to his heels.

A lady residing on Prospect street, (whose name we have) during the absence of her husband last week, went to the street door at nine o'clock in the evening, and saw the white figure standing at her gate. She closed the door and fainted.

We mention the above names as veritable sources respecting the actual presence of this fellow on the street, and shall be glad to hear from others in still further confirmation of the fact. The above named are all inoffensive persons, who were unarmed and unaware, and it is probable that upon these the fellow hits to practice his tricks. Can he not be apprehended?

The most plausible theory we have heard in explanation of the mystery, is that it is a lunatic, escaped from the Newburgh Asylum[63] some three months since. We have heard it stated, but cannot vouch for the truth, that this lunatic when at the Asylum delighted in disguising himself in a white sheet, frightening his keepers and those about the Asylum. It is supposed, with the sagacity possessed by many lunatics, he manages to secrete himself in some of the vaults of the cemetery during the day, merely venturing out at night. The fact that while a party one night gave chase, he scaled the fence of the Erie street cemetery and disappeared, would warrant this belief. Those who have met this "ghost," speak of its peculiar and cat-like movement, which is often a peculiarity of lunatics.

The theory that an organized band of persons is prowling about the city, with white sheets under their garments, only to be used when occasion offers, is hardly probable, as no attempt at robbery has thus far been made by the apparition, and it is hardly supposable that any one with a sane mind would take his life in hand and brave the organized patrols that are now known to be on the constant look-out, and who are fully prepared to meet his ghost-ship with cold lead.—*Cleve. Review.*

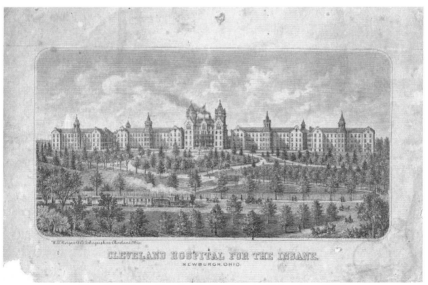

Cleveland State Hospital in Newburgh, Ohio, circa 1875.

---

[63] The Newburgh Asylum opened in 1855, the asylum was later renamed the Cleveland State Hospital. In 1977 the building was demolished. For more information on the history of the hospital see https://clevelandhistorical.org/items/show/576 (accessed August 12, 2018).

Muscatine Weekly Journal, Muscatine, Iowa,
April 5, 1861, pg. 1.

GEN. JACKSON TALKS THROUGH THE SPIRITS.—
Mrs. Cora L.V. Hatch,[64] the medium, has been speaking for Gen.
Jackson's[65] ghost. He says he now regrets that he did not carry
into execution a purpose which would probably have removed the
seeds of the present discord, by which he means hanging the
traitors.[66] He is opposed to any compromise.

The Daily Exchange, Baltimore, Maryland,
April 6, 1861, pg. 1.

Two of the night watchman at Cleveland were frightened
and ran like hares, a few nights ago, at the sight of what they
supposed to be a ghost, but which was only an anxious mother, in
her night dress, hurrying to call a physician for her sick child.

Evening Star, Washington, DC,
May 6, 1861, pg. 2.

A supposed ghost at St. Louis tumbled head foremost down
some stairs where it was cutting up some pranks, and produced
very unspiritual racket and groans. The alarming apparition turned
out to be a young man, who had tangled his feet in the white sheet
he had wrapped around him. He will not soon attempt such sport
again.

---

[64] Cora L. V. Hatch (1840-1923) was a popular and successful
Spiritualist medium.
[65] Andrew Jackson (1767-1845) was president of the United States
from 1829-1837.
[66] In 1832-1833, President Jackson faced the Nullification Crisis
between South Carolina and the federal government.

The Mountainer, Great Salt Lake City, Utah
Territory, May 11, 1861, pg. 1.

HAUNTED—Paris letters state that the ghost of the
Duchess d'Able walks—and is frightening the Empress Eugenie[67]
into her grave. Masses and vigils seem powerless against the
phantom.

The Pacific Commercial Advertiser, Honolulu, Oahu,
Hawaiian Islands, June 6, 1861, pg. 4.

A Haunted House in Indianapolis

The Indianapolis *Journal* tells of a friend who had to go a
house hunting, and after a weary search for several days was upon
the point of giving up the chase for a suitable domicile, and had
about made up his mind to either take up his quarters in the county
poor house or at the Bates House, when lo! the sign "For Rent"
struck his vision from the window of a two story house on
Mississippi street. It was a house of ordinary appearance outside,
but on going in a queer sort of feeling took hold of our friend. It
seemed to him that the sign was a lie, that the house was already
occupied, but he rubbed his eyes and saw clearly that the rooms
were as empty as [a] cuckoo's nest in March, so he rented the
house and moved into it. From that day to this he has been living
with a ghost! When he passes through the house a feeling of
something or somebody behind him or about him pervades his
senses.

There are certain doors in the house that, no matter how
well fastened they may be, are opened and shut at pleasure by an
unseen power, and on one occasion that the ghost was seen to pass
out through a bolted door. Members of the household have
frequently felt the grasp of his ghostship and screamed for

---

[67] Empress Eugenie de Montijo (1826-1920) was the last empress of
France.

assistance. Night after night all the noise of the family household would be performed by the ghost, and the most careful scrutiny revealed nothing disturbed. Not long since the noises from midnight until 3 o'clock were all those incident to the packing and moving of household goods. The boxes were packed with dishes and tin ware, the lid nailed down and the boxes rolled out. Our gloomy friend fairly danced for joy at the parting, but his happiness was but short duration, for not many nights afterwards the ghost moved back into his old quarters. Since then he has been house hunting. When he told the story, the big drops of perspiration stood upon his forehead, and he fairly trembled at the idea of being compelled to guard his family another night in the haunted house.

The Ottawa Free Trader, Ottawa, Illinois, October 12, 1861, pg. 2.

A GHOST STORY.—Missionary Wolff tells a story of a certain M. Priegweg, of Geneva, a good and excellent Christian, to whom a ghost appeared as he was going to bed, and said, "I am the ghost of a person who was hanged here six weeks ago." "That's no business of mine," replied Preigweg; "so good night."

Cleveland Morning Leader, Cleveland, Ohio,] October 14, 1861, pg. 3.

THE GHOST.—The contemptible villain who last winter and spring frightened half of Cleveland by appearing in the *role* of a ghost upon sundry streets, has opened on another with the same game. A gentleman walking along Seneca street, between St. Clair and Lake, about 8 o'clock last evening, saw his ghostship emerge from a blind alley. Now, if this trifling with the feelings of others resulted merely in startling a few men, it would still be reprehensible, but when it is considered that women and children have been frightened to death by such apparitions, it becomes a serious matter, and no mercy should be shown the culprit. He deserves to be knocked down, spitted upon a bayonet, or shot like a dog, and the man who will do this will receive the thanks of the community. We will warrant that cold lead, or a sound hickory club will find something more tangible to operate upon than thin air.

Cleveland Morning Leader, Cleveland, Ohio, October 14, 1861, pg. 4.

THE "CLEVELAND GHOST." GONE TO HARRISBURG, PA.—The Ghost referred to below is no doubt the same as created so much excitement in this city last spring. The Pittsburgh Chronicle has the following:

A GHOST TROUBLE.—An itinerant ghost of variable form and size, has been troubling the denizens of Harrisburg for several nights past. Last Thursday night, a young man was walking up Third street, when he suddenly beheld the ghost in a field to his right. The figure, he says, was ten feet high, and moved smoothly and noiselessly along. The young man remembered nothing more until he found himself lying on the ground, the ghost no where to be seen.

Richmond Enquirer, Richmond, Virginia, November 8, 1861, pg. 4.

There is but one regiment of troops in Alexandria, and of these, seven companies are quartered in the Marshall House.[68]

---

[68] The Marshall House Hotel was the site of Col. Elmer Ellsworth's death on May 24, 1861. Following the occupation of Alexandria, Virginia by Union forces, Col. Ellsworth removed a Confederate flag from the hotel's roof. Hotel owner James W. Jackson fatally shot Ellsworth and was then killed by one

Some time ago a New Jersey regiment, which was quartered in the same building, made a curious exhibitions of themselves. About midnight they stampeded from the premises in great terror, declaring that they had seen Jackson's ghost![69] And no persuasions or ridicule could remove the impressions or induce them to return to the building.

Daily Dispatch, Richmond, Virginia, November 27, 1861, pg. 1.

ARMY OF THE POTOMAC
[OUR OWN CORRESPONDENT]

DUMFRIES, Nov. 22, 1861.

Lying in a small valley which stretches to the Potomac and nearly surrounded by a range of hills, is what remains of the old colonial town of Dumfries, the point from which your correspondent is now writing. Entering on the Brentsville road, one passes over a sandy and rolling tract of country, and comes to a terrace, if one may so call the ridge that rises abruptly from the valley, which completely overlooks the town, and gives a good panoramic view of the stream upon which it is situated. Stretching out in a southerly direction, widening gradually in its course is Quantico creek, and beyond it the Potomac, a silver-like thread of water, just visible between the headlands at the mouth of the bay. Still farther on, the shore of Maryland is visible, dotted here and there with farmhouses and patches of woodland, its line of hills forming the distant horizon. The land around Dumfries is generally poor, and covered with a dense growth of young pines, or with forests of

---

of Ellsworth's soldiers.

[69] The Marshall House was demolished in the 1950s and the site is now a boutique hotel. The site of the Marshall House is rumored to be haunted. Guests have reported hearing gunshots and seeing balls of light floating through the halls.

stinted oak, showing it has at sometime in its history been cleared land. Coming in from the North, winding between the hills and dashing over the rocks in hundreds of miniature cascades, the Quantico enters the town, and passes out of it through a marsh, or meadow, half a mile in length. From this point it grows wider and deeper, until it runs into the Potomac at Evansport.

The town itself is built upon a side hill, which slopes gradually to the water. Coming into it, the first house visible is upon an eminence called "Rose Hill," from which a splendid view is obtained. It is an old house that has been for some time deserted, a legend hanging about it of a poor suicide, who blew his brains out within its walls, and whose ghost still lingers around the place. Every old town has its haunted spot—the point of interest to strangers and its bugbear for children—and Dumfries is no exception to the rule. Unfortunately, the army was in need of boards,

ARMY OF THE POTOMAC.

[OUR OWN CORRESPONDENT.]

DUMFRIES, Nov. 22, 1861.

Lying in a small valley which stretches to the Potomac and nearly surrounded by a range of hills, is what remains of the old colonial town of Dumfries, the point from within your correspondent is now writing. Entering on the Brentsville road, one passes over a sandy and rolling tract of country, and comes to a terrace, if one may so call the ridge that rises abruptly from the valley, which completely overlooks the town, and gives a good panoramic view of the stream upon which it is situated. Stretching out in a southerly direction, widening gradually in its course is Quantico creek, and beyond it the Potomac, a silver-like thread of water, just visible between the headlands at the mouth of the bay. Still farther on, the shore of Maryland is visible, dotted here and there with farm-houses and patches of woodland, its line of hills forming the distant horizon. The land around Dumfries is generally poor, and covered with a dense growth of young pines, or with forests of stinted oak, showing it has at some time in its history been cleared land. Coming in from the North, winding between the hills and dashing over the rocks in hundreds of miniature cascades, the Quantico enters the town, and passes out of it through a marsh, or meadow, half a mile in length. From this point it grows wider and deeper, until it runs into the Potomac at Evansport.

and this house has been stripped completely, and now little but the framework remains to hold the dead man's spirit. It was near sunset when I rode up the hill, and standing beside the haunted building got an idea of the scenery which I am trying to express in words. The evening wind sighed through the bare rafters like the moaning of some restless spirt, and a night owl flew out of a broken window and flitted into the dark shadow of some neighboring pines. Built by a man of wealth and influence,

"The house remain'd awhile,
Silent and tenantless—then
went to stranger."[70]—

Since then it has passed through years of neglect, and has now gone to ruin and decay. To those who are fond of relics of the past the spot was of interest, and one could imagine more old wives' tales hanging about it than pine cones in the forest. Standing beside it, many a delicious memory floats through the mind like the dream of some long-forgotten melody, and the brain is filled with weird and mystical recollections of long ago….

Lewistown Gazette, Lewistown, Pennsylvania, December 4, 1861, pg. 3.

Fatal Fear of Ghosts.

A very sad and fatal accident occurred at a ladies school in Montreal, on Friday last. During the lunch hour, several of the boarders and scholars were in the school room, chatting and telling stories. The conversation fell upon ghosts, and one of the young disputants—a fine girl, thirteen years of age—said warmly, and loudly, that before a ghost should catch her, she would throw herself out of a window, on the sill of which she was sitting. The preceptress, who was in the room at the time, tapped her desk as a warning to make less noise, when this unfortunate young lady, startled by the noise, or her nervous system terribly worked upon, fell or threw herself out of the window, and died the next morning.

---

[70] From the poem "The House of Mourning" by Ebenezer Mack published in *The Cat-Fight; A Mock Heroic Poem* (New York, 1824).

Mineral Point Weekly Tribune, Mineral Point, Wisconsin, December 17, 1861, pg. 1.

PHOTOGRAPHS OF GHOSTS.—The *London Review*, in an article on the tendency in modern literature to the revival of ghost stories, suggests to the writers as a verification, that they obtain photographs of their special visitors. It says:—"Now, if the specter can ask the favor, let science do its turn. Let optics and chemistry catch this modern ghost and photograph it! It can fix the tails of comets and the atmosphere of the sun; the other day a photographer at Berlin caught a stream of electric light flowing out of the bronze spear of Kiss "Amazon." A ghost can be hardly less material, if it wears crinoline,[71] is helped twice to beef, drinks claret and wants a portrait taken. The photographer's plate is liable to no delusions, has no brains to be diseased, and is exact in its testimony.[72]

---

[71] A crinoline is a stiff hooped petticoat that gave the bell shape in women's clothing of the 1860s.

[72] Spirit photography would emerge during this period. William H. Mumler (1832-1884) is credited with taking the first spirit photograph. For more about William H. Mumler and spirit photography see Peter Manseau *The Apparitionists: A Tale of Phantoms, Fraud, Photography, and the Man Who Captured Lincoln's Ghost* (New York: Houghton Mifflin Harcourt, 2017).

1862

St. Mary's Beacon, Leonard Town, Maryland, January 2, 1862, pg. 1.

HAUNTED HOUSES.

Forty years have passed since the memorable; "Purrington Tragedy" convulsed the good people of Maine.[73] Purrington was a laboring man in humble circumstance, residing in the suburbs of Augusta, the capital, and was generally regarded as a quiet, honest, and goodhearted man. His family consisted of a wife and seven children, six of whom were girls. For some time he had been desponding, and often expressed a fear that his family would come to want. One morning he arose early and read his Bible, leaving it open at the chapter narrating Abraham's attempted sacrifice of his son. Securing an axe, he entered his bedroom, where he had left his wife sleeping, and killed her with a single blow. His two eldest daughters were next murdered by repeated strokes, and he followed up the horrid butchery by killing those of his other children who slept on the same floor. He then ascended to the chamber where his only son was sleeping, and struck at him with

---

[73] James Purrington murdered his family on July 9, 1806. For more on the Purrington Tragedy see
https://touringmaineshistory.wordpress.com/2012/03/02/the-purrinton-tragedy-augusta-1806/ (accessed August 14, 2018).

the axe, inflicting a terrible wound. The youth, however, succeeded in getting up and springing out of the window before the blow could be repeated, and hastened to a neighbor's for assistance. When help arrived, Purrington was found dead in the kitchen, his throat cut from ear to ear, a blood-stained razor in his hand, and his wife and entire family, save the son, lying dead in the rooms around him. On the wall, over the mantelpiece, was the full imprint of the wretched man's right hand, as if he had staggered forward cutting his throat, and caught thus at the wall for support. He was buried in a dishonored grave at the crossing of four roads, without coffin or prayer, after the ancient mode of disposing of suicides and murderers. His victims were interred in the burial-ground, and another family moved into the premises—the scene of the dreadful tragedy. But the house did not long remained tenanted. Rumors of its being haunted soon were afloat; not a door could be kept shut; strange noises were heard, and no amount of scrubbing could remove the imprint of that bloody hand from the wainscot. The house finally fell into ruins, and was eventually razed to the ground a few years ago, and its site is now a cornfield.

There has also been, within a few years, another haunted house in Augusta, standing on Bridge street, on the north side of the way. This house stood unoccupied for years; its reputation being such that no one desired to rent or buy it. The owner finally found a family up country willing to take possession of the tenement, and they arrived with their load of furniture about the middle of the afternoon. A few things were removed from the cart, enough to get a hasty dinner and set a table, and the family seated

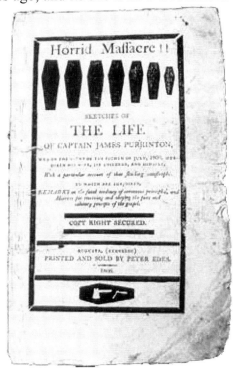

themselves to the repast. While eating and chattering, a strange groan was heard, and an awful apparition came up from the cellar—the head and shoulders of a man without the body—which slowly circulated around the table, and then disappeared down the cellar-way. Of course the family did not remove any more of their furniture from the cart, and stayed only long enough to gather their property, when they hastily departed, returning to the place from whence they came. This house is still unoccupied, and rapidly falling into decay.

In the western part of Gardiner, a village eight miles south of Augusta, is a little cottage, which has long borne the reputation of a haunted house. This cottage had been owned by a sailor, who went off to sea, and was supposed to have been lost overboard, shipwrecked, or murdered, as he was never heard from after his departure. In the course of time it became the belief of the vicinity that this sailor's spirit was haunting the premises; a shadow being repeatedly seen by the several members of the family occupying the house. It was quite a harmless manifestation, however, the shadow generally appearing near the gate, and quietly approaching the house—often causing the occupants to think that visitors were coming, but always "dissolving into thin air" before it reached the front door.

Our informant was once visiting at this cottage when the shadow was seen by the eldest daughter, and declares that the entire family had no doubts of the supernatural origin of the apparition, although it had been seen so often that no emotion was caused by its visit.

Not many years ago, an old house, standing between Albany and Schenectady, on the turnpike road, was said to be subject to ghostly visitations. Lights were seen at unusual hours, and strange noises were heard. The place had begun to acquire considerable reputation as a haunted house, when some astute officials made a secret descent upon it, and arrested quite a number of counterfeiters, whose occupancy and occupation fully explained the ghostly phenomena which had been seen.

Near the road which winds along the foot of Mount Royal, two miles from Montreal, there stands a house which is regarded as haunted by all superstitious people in the neighborhood. It was formerly the abode of an eccentric old Frenchman, who committed suicide, and about whose character and history a great deal of mystery had gathered.

His body lay several days in the house after his tragical end, before his suicide became known. It is said that the ghost of the suicide is often seen flitting about the premises, with its wild eyes and wilder laugh.

Between Hallowell and Gardiner there stood on a little creek, some thirty years ago, an old mill. The proprietor had been found murdered in the stream below the mill, and it was said that his spirit lingered round the mill. The old residents thereabouts still love to dwell upon the mystery.

Apropos of this subject, there is not far from Hempstead, L.I., an inlet in a small river called "Lover's Creek," and the name thus originated: A young man, who was devotedly attached to a fair young girl near, had become jealous of her unconscious coquetry, and is supposed to have given her an instant and fatal poison, as she was found dead, without external marks of violence, while the lover lay near, cold and motionless, with a discharged pistol in his right hand, and a bullet buried in his brain. Another account is that the maiden suddenly died of some obscure and deadly disease, and the lover, through grief and despair, perhaps coupled with a fear of being thought her murderer, shot himself on the spot where lay her lifeless form. This latter account is more generally favored, for, it is said, the lovers are often seen walking on the shore, or sailing about the river in a spectral boat, and otherwise living out, in ghostly form, the existence whose earthly career was interrupted in such a melancholy manner.

Near Belladona, N.Y., there is an old farmhouse which stands deserted. The former owner poisoned his wife, as was generally supposed, though no legal evidence was produced in support of the prevailing suspicion. The suspected party suddenly removed to the west, but not before the rumor became currant that he had been frightened nearly out of his senses by repeated visits from the spirit of his wife. The house having acquired a bad name, it was easy for the more superstitious portions of the community to find mysteries and wonders to keep up its reputation.

It is probable that most of the alleged hauntings could be explained on natural principles, were the plain truth to be known. It must be conceded, however, that there have been such accumulations of evidence respecting ghostly visitations as to stagger reason and challenge belief. Nearly every mysterious and unexplained murder becomes the subject of superstitious interest and gossip, until guesses and suspicious grow to revelations, and the commonest sights and sounds become portents of horror. There is, moreover, associated with the rude and popular sense of justice, a natural desire that the secret murder should be haunted— that buried bones and unavenged blood should be brought up in judgment against the guilty party; and it may be this creditable abhorrence of wickedness that causes all tales of supernatural vengeance and ghostly pursuit to be so well received by all classes and conditions of society.

Daily Morning News, Savannah, Georgia, February 18, 1862, pg. 2.

[Correspondence of the Petersburg Express.]
Interesting Conversation with Released Hatteras Prisoners—
Interesting Facts Gleaned, etc.

NORFOLK, February 13, 1862.

We had the pleasure of conversing with one of the prisoners recently arrived in our city from Fort Warren.[74] He was captured at Hatteras, and resides in Washington, N.C. We give his statement:

…Some of the Yankee soldiers swear to our men that they had been visited by rebel ghosts that died at Fort Warren.[75] Our boys laughed heartily over the joke, but they stick to it as truth.

---

[74] Fort Warren is located in Boston, Massachusetts and during the Civil War housed Confederate POWS. Fort Warren gained a reputation for the harsh treatment of prisoners.

[75] During the war, Union soldiers reported seeing spirits of dead prisoners. Legend holds that Fort Warren is haunted by several restless spirits including the Lady in Black.

Bellows Falls Times, Bellows Falls, Vermont,
May 23, 1862, pg. 2.

The cell at the Tombs at New York,[76] where the slaver Gordon[77] was confined previous to his execution, has been haunted ever since so that no prisoner dared to stay there. The "ghost" has just been found out to be a man in the cell above, who moaned through a crack between the two cells. There will be no more mysterious noise there.

White Cloud Kansas Chief, White Cloud, Kansas,
August 7, 1862, pg. 1.

THE SEVEN LOST BRIDES.
A LEGENED OF NEW ORLEANS.

In the upper part of New Orleans, not far from the Mississippi river, stands an old house, well known in that part of the city as the "haunted house." It is said that no tenant can be induced to remain long in it; but all, disturbed by supernatural sights and sounds, speedily seek another dwelling. These

---

[76] The Tombs refers to the Manhattan Detention Complex, New York City's notorious jail.

[77] Nathaniel Gordon (1826-1862) was the only slave trader to be tried and executed for being engaged in the slave trade under the Piracy Law of 1820.

nocturnal disturbances are sufficiently explained—to some at least—by the following legend:

"Long time ago," long before New Orleans was a great city, and when the quarter now named Lafayette was occupied by cane-fields and partly by marshes, the old house—old even then—stood, as now, not far from the bank of the river, and, unsurrounded by blocks and squares of substantial buildings, as to-day, was the centre of a plantation, and was haunted only by sunny faces and merry voices. Its owner was an old gentleman, a widower, who had seven treasures in seven daughters—all beautiful, intelligent and amiable.

When the oldest daughter was at an age to marry, she was wooed and won by a young planter in the neighborhood, and for once the course of true love seemed to run smooth.

All parties were agreed as to the suitability of the match, and when the wedding night arrived, willing guests flocked from all quarters to honor the occasion. The old house was brilliantly illuminated, and the sounds of music and of dancing echoed through its chambers. In short, everything went merrily onward, and gay Louisiana never saw a gayer assemblage.

But all this merriment was doomed to meet a strange and sudden end.

Scarcely had the nuptial benediction been pronounced, when it was observed that the bride was missing. The evening passed on, and she did not return. Wonder was followed by fear, and search was made through the house and grounds, and finally through the neighborhood, but all without success.

All that night, and for days and weeks after, the search was continued with all the sleepless energy and vigilance which love could prompt, but all in vain; not the slightest trace was ever found of the missing bride.

Had she, in some sudden aberration of mind, wandered into the boundless swamps and perished miserably of hunger and exposure? Or had she some fearful and unbosomed grief, which had caused her to cast herself into the turbid waters of the Mississippi? Or had she, perchance, met and loved some person so far beneath her in station as to render an open union hapless, and they had fled together to distant lands?

Such was some of the conjectures of the gossips concerning her fate; while others told dreary stories of the dreadful and desperate deeds of the pirates of the Gulf; or late nights with terrified glances cast over the shoulders, toward the door, whispered ghastly tales of the doings of the demon huntsman, whose horn was often heard among the woods and marches, and the baying of whose dogs, mingled with the rustling of the wind among the leaves, as it struck upon his ear in the dreary hours of night, caused many a pious Arcadian to hastily cross himself and utter an *Ave Maria*, and a petition for protection against the devil and all his angels.

Select Tale.

THE SEVEN LOST BRIDES.

A LEGEND OF NEW ORLEANS.

In the upper part of New Orleans, not far from the Mississippi river, stands an old house, well known in that part of the city as the "haunted house." It is said that no tenant can be induced to remain long in it; but all, disturbed by supernatural sights and sounds, speedily seek another dwelling. These nocturnal disturbances are sufficiently explained—to some at least—by the following legend: "Long time ago," long before New Orleans was a great city, and when the quarter now named Lafayette was occupied by cane-fields and partly by marshes, the old house—old, even then—stood, as now, not far from the bank of the river, and, unsurrounded by blocks and squares of substantial buildings, as to-day, was the centre of a plantation, and was haunted only by sunny faces and merry voices. Its owner was an old gentleman, a widower, who had seven treasures in seven daughters—all beautiful, intelligent and amiable.

It would be tedious to tell—as to hear, save in the briefest manner—how, one after another, five more of the seven daughters disappeared in the same way—each on their wedding night—till one was left, the youngest, the most beautiful, the best beloved of all. A strange infatuation seemed to enchain all who were concerned; and while, when each was lost, the same frantic search, of wild grief, and of despairing acquiescence was enacted, none ever dreamed of making the mysterious fate which seemed to hang over the family, on objection to the marriage of the young girl. And thus it came to pass that the last daughter became betrothed, as the rest had been, to one well worthy of her; and in due time, another large company assembled to grace the nuptials.

But on this occasion there was but little merriment. The guests clustered together in groups of two and threes, and in whispers spoke of the lost sisters. All seemed to feel as though they were shadowed by the wings of some dark and terrible

92

misfortune hovering over the doomed house. No one was found bold enough to utter a jest, or speak a gay thoughtless word.

In the meantime, all possible care was taken to guard the bride from the fate of her sisters. A chosen body of friends watched over her, and never permitted her to be absent from their sights.

Thus were matters situated, when the hour appointed for the nuptial ceremony arrived.

But the final vows was scarcely spoken, when the sound of a distant horn was heard, and a thrill of terror struck to each heart.

It approached nearer and nearer, till at last the heavy tramp of a man, accompanied by the pattering sound of the feet of hurrying dogs, was heard upon the rotunda. All eyes were fixed upon the closed door. It opened with a crash, and a gigantic huntsman, clad in green and surrounded by a pack of huge and panting hounds, stood upon the threshold. Fixed to their places, the visitors stared with glassy eyes upon the terrible visitor, and awaited with speechless terror his further movement. Fixing his flashing eyes upon the bride, with imperial dignity, he raised his right hand toward her. With tottering steps she advanced and fell fainting in his arms. One blast up on his mighty horn, one yell from the ferocious pack, and the green huntsman sprang from the house, bearing with him the inanimate form of the doomed bride. Fainter and fainter grew the sound of the dogs, till they faded quite away in the distance; and then, and not till then, did the beholders of this strange scene recover from the spell which had deprived them of the power of speaking or moving.

All those who were present at this supernatural abduction, have long since mingled their ashes with parent earth, but the old house still stands, a witness to the truth of the legend; and on stormy nights, the demon huntsman's horn, and the baying of his dogs, rising above the roaring tempest, may be heard sounding along the Metairie Ridge, and through the swamps and woods adjoining; and at midnight hour the ghost of the bereaved old father yet wanders through the deserted chambers of the ancient house, weeping and wringing his shadowy hands, and repeating, in agonizing tones, the names of the seven lost brides.

Chicago Daily Tribune, Chicago, Illinois, August 13, 1862, pg. 2.

OUR ST. LOUIS LETTER
[Special Correspondence of the Chicago Tribune.]

ST. LOUIS, August 11, 1862.

…The Irish residents in the vicinity of Fifteenth and Biddle streets in this city, have been terribly excited for several nights past, by the reported appearance of a ghost or ghostess. As many as 1,500 person were on the watch on Friday night, and the "locals" are to-day reveling in fun occasioned by the excitement. The *Democrat* of this morning says a six-pounder was loaded and drawn to the vicinity to be discharged at his ghostship—a very dangerous way of getting rid of the nightly visitor—a couple of stout policemen would do the job.

The Nashville Daily Union, Nashville, Tennessee, August 23, 1862, pg. 1.

Some old author gives an account of a battle in which the two opposing armies fought until the whole of both were killed, and, after that, the ghosts of the fallen were seen standing up in full armor and fighting on throughout the rest of the day.

Daily Morning News, Savannah, Georgia,
October 2, 1862, pg. 1.

A GHOST.—The citizens of Lynchburg[78] have been thrown into a fever of excitement by the appearance of a ghost in their midst. It has appropriately selected a deserted hospital as the scene of its nocturnal visitations. The *Republican* gives the following account of the phantom, and experiments upon the structure of the same by civilians and military gentlemen:

On another occasion a large cane in the hand of one of the party present, who made a lick with it at the ghost, passed through the apparition without disturbing it in the least, and struck the wall with a heavy rebound. These facts seem to be well attested, and we are told that nightly a crowd assembles to catch a glimpse of the vagaries of this dead man who revisits the pale lights of the stars. The scene of his perambulations is on the shed of a house back of the Express office, belonging to the late Warwick Hospital, now not used.

Its appearance was as if it arose from behind the chimney, which springs from the roof of the house, and it disappears at the same point. It cannot be the ghost of Hamlet's father, for many of our readers have seen *that* ghost disappear time and time again beneath the floor of the stage of a theatre. Mayhap it may be the ghost of Banquo; but there are many who believe it to be the ghost of some poor solider, many a one having died at the hospital.

The Nashville Daily Union, Nashville, Tennessee,
October 2, 1862, pg. 2.

---

[78] Virginia

A preacher of the M.E. Church says that he and his brethren will fight the rebels in this world, and, if God permit, chase their frightened ghosts in the next.

Daily Morning News, Savannah, Georgia, October 6, 1862, pg. 1.

The Ghost Again.

We mentioned on Friday morning the fact that the ghost of some disembodied spirit visited the vicinity of the late Warwick House Hospital and accounted for the apparition upon the supposition that the shape thus seen was the shadow of some person retiring for the night, which was reflected upon the place, and gave rise to the notion of its being a "spirit." Since the appearance of our article, the locality has been carefully examined, with a view to discover the correctness of our way of accounting for the phantom, and we are

Lynchburg, Virginia, circa 1873

informed by responsible gentlemen that it cannot be correct. This being the case, then, we must confess ourselves non-plussed, and join in with the general opinion that the form thus seen is nothing more nor less than the veritable ghost of some departed one, which revisits the earth for some cause as yet undetermined. As we stated previously, a sword has been passed through the shape, and it has been stricken with a heavy stick, without the least effect, which facts, coming well attested, as they do, assures us of its [unclear].

We, however, are constrained to say that it is a most sensible ghost, for, upon its appearing on Friday night, in its accustomed place, one of the young men present proposed to borrow a pistol, with the purpose of trying the effect of cold lead upon the intangible substance, whereupon it quickly vanished [from] sight, and was not seen for a considerable time afterwards. This fact may serve to aid in the elucidation of the mystery, and the clue which it affords should be followed up. The apparition is described as being the size of an ordinary man, dressed in a long robe or shroud of snowy white, and on Friday it appeared as with the right arm severed from the body at the shoulder. It was witnessed by a large number of persons, and some of them with whom we have conversed, have not yet gotten over their fright. A silver bullet is said to be the only kind that will carry death to a "speret," and it would be a good idea to try the effect upon it. We have received an invitation, from parties who have witnessed the supernatural appearance, to accompany them on a visit to it to-night if it is not "kilt" in the meantime. They promised us to inform it on Saturday night that the Local of the Republican would call on it at that time, and we doubt not that it will do its best and receive us with proper honors. We shall report the result of our visit, if we are not so pleased with our new acquaintance as to make a trip with it to its home in the land of ghosts, wherever that may be.—*Lynchburg Republican.*

Joliet Signal, Joliet, Illinois, October 7, 1862, pg. 1.

A Ghost Story.

A lady, the wife of a wealthy merchant, died recently after a protracted illness; and on the evening of her decease, her husbands, desirous to pass a solitary hour with the body, sent the nurse (who was watching besides the corpse) out of the room. Before the expiration of an hour, the bell by which the deceased had been in habit of summoning the nurse, rang violently, and the woman, fancying the unfortunate widower was taken suddenly ill, hurried into the room.

He dismissed her angrily, at the same time protesting that he had not rung.—Shortly afterward, the bell was rung a second time, when the woman observed to one of the servants that she should attend to the summons as the gentleman might again repent having summoned her, and dismiss her ungraciously.

"It cannot be my master who is ringing now," replied the servant, "for I have this moment left him in the drawing-room."

And when he was still speaking, the bell of the chamber of death rang a third time, and still more violently than before.

The nurse was literally afraid to obey the summons; nor was it till several of the servants agreed to accompany her that she could command sufficient courage. At length they ventured to open the door, expecting to discover within some terrible spectacle.

All, however, was perfectly tranquil; the corpse extended upon the bed under the Holland sheet, which was evidently undisturbed. Such, however, was the agitation of the poor nurse that nothing would induce her to remain alone with the body; and one of the house maids accordingly agreed to become her companion in the adjoining dressing-room.

They had not been there many minutes when the bell again sounded; nor could there be any mistake on the subject, for the bell wire passing round the dressing-room was in motion, and the servants in the offices could see the vibration of the bell. The family butler accordingly determined to support the courage of the terrified women, by accompanying them back to the dressing-room, in which they were to sit with the door open, so as to command a view of the bed.

These precaution effectually unraveled the mystery. A string had been attached to the bell pull, to enable the sick lady to summon her attendants without changing her position which string still unmoved, hung down upon the floor, and a favorite kitten, that was often admitted into the room to amuse the invalid, having entered the chamber unobserved, was playing with the string and becoming entangled in pussy's feet had produced the panic that had caused the hearts of the maidens to tremble.

But for the courage of the butler, and for this fortunate explanations, the family mansion would have been classed among the list of haunted houses, and probably deserted, until it became dismantled and ruined.

The Tri-Weekly Telegraph, Houston, Texas, October 20, 1862, pg. 2.

The people of Lynchburg, Va., are quite excited by the appearance of a real bona fide, genuine ghost in that city. It has been run through with a sword, divided with a stick and beaten with a cane, all to no purpose, very many people have seen it.

Southern Confederacy, Atlanta, Georgia, November 6, 1862, pg. 2.

Singular Phenomenon

The "local" of the Petersburg *Express* of the 31 October, is responsible for the following.

A gentleman called our attention yesterday to the existence of very singular phenomenon about his shoulder, which a number of persons have examined into, but which none of them are able to explain. Just at the juncture of the arm with the body, a noise, as distinct, but much more rapid, and exactly resembling the ticking of a watch, is constantly heard. So distinct indeed, it is, that a person standing with his ear at the distance of a foot from the gentleman's shoulder, can readily hear it. It cannot be produced by the coursing of the blood through the veins or arteries, for we should think that the rapidity of the "ticking" would be regulated by the beating of the heart, and they outnumber the heart's contraction five or ten to one.—It is an inexplicable mystery both to the gentleman himself and to all who have examined the case. The "ticking" noise only made its appearance within the past three or four days.

We have a distinct recollection of the perpetration of the "local" of the Lynchburg *Republican* about the Ghost. We mention this to let the "local" of our Virginia exchanges know that hereafter we shall receive their marvelous reports for just what they are worth.

Wytheville Dispatch, Wytheville, Virginia, November 25, 1862, pg. 1.

The Ghost on Tye River.

MR. EDITOR:—A few nights ago while walking on the banks of Tye River, I observed a boat containing a single occupant, shoot out from a dark cave on the opposite side and pass slowly down the center of the stream towards James River. The circumstance appearing rather suspicious to my mind I took the liberty of hailing the nocturnal craft, when to my utter surprise the occupant arose in the middle of the boat and presented his breast to my view. He was of gigantic size, and was in a perfect state of nudity. I asked him from whence he came and whither he was going? For sometime he did not seem disposed to answer my question, but at length replied in the following strain: "Biped of earth, I am here for justice, and shall remain until earth swallows up thieves of the land." I then asked him if he was not the ghost who had recently visited Lynchburg? "I am biped, he replied." What did you visit Lynchburg for? I asked. "I visited Lynchburg for the purpose of communicating with some friends of earth, but the extortions of the place robbed me of all the earthly good I had about me, even the clothes on my back, and then tried to kill me by shooting an earthly ball through my body—but I escaped, thank the father of Ghosts, and am now on my way to the capitol, where I am told that the extortioners are a very liberal set of fellows, only stealing everything but the under clothes on a man.—Good-bye, biped," and off went the ghost, boat and all in a cloud of smoke.

The banks of the Tye River will be thronged with people to-morrow night, expecting to see what is left of the ghost after passing the ordeal of the thieves of Richmond.

Cleveland Morning Leader, Cleveland, Ohio, November 26, 1862, pg. 3.

AFTER HIM.—The ghost has again become the exciting topic of conversation.—Speculation is rife with regard to who the individual is. All agree that if he isn't a ghost he ought to be. We are informed that a party, well armed with clubs and revolvers, patrolled Erie street and vicinity last night, in hopes of meeting him. The ghost didn't find it convenient to walk, however, owning probably to the "inclemency of the weather."

Cleveland Morning Leader, Cleveland, Ohio, November 26, 1862, pg. 4.

THE GHOST AFTER A SHAVE.—The "ghost" has heretofore confined his pranks to the vicinity of Erie street, but last night we heard of him as far down as the American House. He made an unceremonious entrance into Ambush's barber shop, beneath the American, about ten o'clock, entering by the back stairs. There were no customers in at that moment, it chanced, and all the hands were out except John Brown the barber. Brown was dozing in a chair, and says the first he know of the presence of the ghost, was his touching him with a clammy hand, which felt like lead.—Brown jumped from the chair as he saw him, his hair standing on end, and exclaimed, "Whofore and whence dost thou? Ha?— Wentest thou from the goings of mortality, or art thou from some heterogeneous people?—Speak." But the ghost didn't speak. He raised a threatening finger and advanced towards him, and John Brown stopped to hold no further converse. John Brown got out of that barber shop very suddenly, and he would be "marching on"[79] at this time, doubtless, had he not been stopped by Ambush on the sidewalk. Brown was too much frightened to speak for some time, but at length said he seen the ghost. On returning to the shop, nothing was seen of his ghostship. He probably came down to be shaved and to have his head "shampooed."

It was doubtless a joke on the part of someone about the American, to frighten Brown. Viewed in that light, it was abundantly successful.

Cleveland Morning Leader, Cleveland, Ohio, November 27, 1862, pg. 4.

THE GHOST ON ERIE STREET.—Our account of the ghost fright which was given a servant girl on Erie street last Monday night, was incorrect in one particular. She did not see the ghost looking out of a window of an unoccupied house which she was passing.—The object looked into her chamber window. The girl, Sarah Gallagher, had just come in from a walk with another

---

[79] This is a play on the lyrics "John Brown's body lies a-moldering in the grave,/His soul's marching on!" from the popular song "John Brown's Body."

girl and both had gone to the former's room, which is the 2d story of the back part of No. 117, Erie street. The roof of a one story kitchen in the rear of her room reaches up to her chamber window. The window was up, and the blinds closed. While the girls were talking together, they heard a slight noise at the window. They looked in that direction and saw the blinds opening, disclosing the figure of a man, all in white, who was standing on the kitchen roof looking in. Sarah gave a shriek and dropped on the floor in convulsions.—Her companion was greatly frightened, but did not lose her presence of mind. She advanced to the window, and says the figure appeared to fall backward and then vanish. The face was pale, and blood seemed to be running from its mouth.

The house was alarmed, and a physician sent for to attend to the girl in convulsions. Throughout the whole night two men were required to hold her, she coming out of one fit to go into another immediately. Whenever her attendant would let go of her hands she would clutch fiercely at her throat. She shrieked continually—"There he is! I see him at the window! take him away, & c." This morning the girl had recovered from the fits, and is becoming composed. The pranks of the ghost came near to costing a life.

Since the above occurrence, Marshal Gallagher is fully aroused to the work of finding out what scoundrel or idiot it is that can find any gratification in going about in ghostly apparel, frightening people out of their senses, and destroying the quiet of peaceful neighborhoods. Strict watches will be set for him, and if seen, the chances are that he will get a bullet through him which will give reality to his present romancing, and make him a ghost indeed. He should be shot with as little remorse as one would shoot a mad dog, and whoever will do it will render community an essential service.

Cleveland Morning Leader, Cleveland, Ohio, December 4, 1862, pg. 3.

THE GHOST.—The report is circulated every day that the "ghost" is caught and is in jail. Although strenuous efforts have been made by the police to detect and arrest the individual who is playing spectre, no one has as yet been arrested. Suspicious attaches to two or three persons as the "ghost," but nothing certain has been ascertained. We hear of a woman who met his ghostship the other night in an alley. She was not frightened, but suspected who it was from the direction in which he came. She told him that she would tell him who he was if he would come to a gaslight. He did so, and her previous suspicion was confirmed. She pronounced his name, and he fled hurriedly. She has sent us his name, but for fear that there may be some mistake about it we withhold it. If this article should meet the eye of the really guilty one, we hope he will cease to "affright the souls of timid adversaries," or any other souls, and thus avoid disagreeable exposures.

Our own theory with regard to the "man in white" has long been that he is some one who is insane, if not in all things, at least on the ghost question. He may be sane on all other subjects, but he is certainly not "sound" on the ghost. We cannot believe that a man could be found to run such risks as he does from a broken head or a bullet, simply for the fun of frightening timid women and children. Time may determine whether our theory is correct or not.

Cleveland Morning Leader, Cleveland, Ohio, December 5, 1862, pg. 3.

THE GHOST DISCOVERED!—Last evening a party of resolute fellows, armed with clubs, bowie-knives and revolvers, started out on a search for the ghost. They patrolled the streets in the vicinity of the cemetery for several hours. About midnight one of the party who had got a little ahead of his fellows, ran back, hatless and pale with fright, exclaiming, "I have seen him! I have seen the Ghost!" His comrades were seized with a sudden trembling and showed a disposition to run. One suddenly remembered an engagement that he had down town and started on a run to fulfill it. Another said that he had been up late for several nights and he "thought he'd go home," and away he scampered also. The remainder held a consultation and concluded to investigate at all hazards. They cocked their revolvers, loosened their knives, and grasping their clubs more firmly, crept stealthily, with chattering teeth, to the spot indicated. They peered through cracks in the fence inclosing the yard, and the horrible spectre was revealed to them, swinging its weird arms in the moonlight, and nodding its head in a most diabolical manner. All immediately took to their heels except one bold fellow who determined to ascertain whether his Ghostship was flesh or blood or not. He sprang over the fence, club in hand.

Erie St. Cemetery (now 9th St.) in Cleveland, Ohio, circa 1860s

The spectre did not retreat but continued to swing its arms and nod its head mockingly. Chocking down his fear the man raised his club resolutely and aimed a crushing blow fairly at the spectre's head. Down went the ghost hunter, for his club met with but little resistance. Horror stricken he regained his feet, when lo! he found that the Ghost was a woman's night gown which had been left out on a clothes line. A night-cap pinned on the line at the top of the garment was what appeared to the excited imagination of the ghost hunters to be the spectre's head. None of that party desire to have the papers say anything about it and they probably wont.

Cleveland Morning Leader, Cleveland, Ohio, December 6, 1862, pg. 3.

A LETTER FROM "MOLLIE."—DEAR MR. EDITOR:— You have entirely miscalculated the danger attending the nightly wanderings of the Erie street Ghost who, be he mortal or "thing of air," is likely to be reckoned among the oldest inhabitants of the city, and will certainly die of old age long before our valiant police can put an end to his unquiet walks! I pray you also dismiss your sympathies in behalf of the "timid women and children," and turn them (where they will not be out of place) upon the gallant braves who sally forth night after night armed to the teeth, in "goodly companie," and keeping up their oozing valor by song and jest, and taking care to announce the plan of their campaign, might chance to be walking that way!

Rest assured if there are any deaths from fright in the city, they will be in the ranks of this brave crew, and not among the "defenseless women and children."

Heaven grant the scoundrel may repent his evil ways and return to daylight and duty, before ever he meets one of our brave police, for the effect of an encounter would certainly be fatal to— the knight of the star!

The Daily Ohio Statesman.

VOL. IX. NO. 155. NEW SERIES. COLUMBUS, OHIO, WEDNESDAY MORNING, DEC. 10, 1862.

Daily Ohio Statesman, Columbus, Ohio, December 10, 1862, pg. 3.

The ghost which has annually returned to plague the Clevelanders has been laid at last. A company of ghost detectives was recently organized, which, after much tribulation, and several stampeded, discovered that the ghost was nothing more than a night shirt and night cap hung out to dry!

Daily Intelligencer, Wheeling, Virginia, December 17, 1862, pg. 3.

A Spook.—For several nights past a certain portion of the city known as East Wheeling, has been very much troubled and disturbed by the nocturnal perambulations of a spook or ghost. This spook assumes all sorts of shapes. It sometimes comes in the shape of a human being, but upon being approached assumes the shape of a cow, or horse, or other animal. His spookship approached a house the other night where a young couple were engaged in the interesting business of courting and the young woman was almost scared out of her wits. The ghost amuses itself almost nightly, by going about peering into people's windows in the middle of the night and frightening women and children. We understand that several attempts have recently been made to capture the thing without success. We shall not be surprised if this ghost shall turn out—like the late Cleveland ghost—to be nothing more than a harmless shirt of chemisette.[80] We shall see.

The Southern Banner, Athens, Georgia, December 17, 1862, pg. 1.

A Ghost Story

We heard one of Gen. McCown's[81] officers tell a hard story on yesterday. It seems that when McCown was in West Tennessee

---

[80] A chemisette is a garment worn to cover the front neckline.
[81] Major General John P. McCown (1815-1879)

this officer was sent into a neighborhood where he was well known. He was riding in a buggy, and overtook an old acquaintance, and friend named Robert Bond. Bond was on foot. The officer, after the usual salutations and inquiry for the news asked Bond to take the buggy and drive on to the next house and await his coming, that he was tired of riding, and wished to walk the intervening half mile. When the officer came to the house the buggy was standing there and the horse tied to the gate.

The officer asked the ladies at the house what had become of Mr. Bond. They amazed, answered that Bond had been killed in a skirmish near Corinth, and that his body had been brought home and buried on the day before the officer arrived.

He asked the ladies who had brought the buggy to the gate. They answered that there was no driver, that the horse came quietly to the enclosure and that one their number had went out and tied him.

Confederate casualties in the Battle of Corinth, 1862

It is needless to state that the officer who made this statement discredits his own sense, but he is confident that he could not have mistaken Bond for another man, that his personal peculiarities were well known to him. But how he could have disappeared, and how a dead man could have driven a horse and buggy, and then vanished, or why his disembodied spirit should have appeared to him when he did not even know that Bond was dead, are questions often asked by the officer referred to.—He is evidently sorely puzzled by the occurrence as were his auditors by its narration—*Knoxville Register*.

Daily Intelligencer, Wheeling, Virginia, December 30, 1862, pg. 3.

A GREAT CIRCULAR GHOST HUNT.—We have heretofore advised our readers that a ghost — a ghastly and horrible ghost — has been perambulating about East Wheeling nearly every night for a couple or three weeks past. Quite a number of persons have seen it and spoken to it and some have thrown stones and brickbats at it. It is a very queer sort of a ghost and seems to have a high regard for its personal comfort. It appears generally about ten o'clock in the evening, with a cowl upon its head like those worn by the members of that ancient and honorable order known as the Sons of Malta.[82] Its person is arrayed in heavy skins and it is said to

---

[82] The Sons of Malta was a fraternal organization during the 19th-century.

present a very *outre*[83] appearance.—Recently it has frightened a great many women and children and has got to be a great nuisance in the particular localities which it chooses to infest. Accordingly a party of ten young men organized themselves into a company of ghost hunters on Saturday night and sallied forth to scour the alleys and byways of East Wheeling. Some with pokers, shovels, clubs, stones and other missiles. They divided the company into couples and searched high and low for the ghost, traversing nearly every alley in that quarter of the town. The hunt was altogether unsuccessful. The ghost got wind of the formidable expedition which had been organized for his extermination and appeared in another section of the city much to the terror of the inhabitants thereof.

The truth about this matter is that some bold fellow whose love of fun outruns his judgement and discretion has been playing ghost with wonderful success and those most immediately interested—those whose families have been frightened and annoyed, in some instances with very serious results—have determined to put an end to his pranks. The ghost generally makes his appearance from the neighborhood of the Government stables, near Hempfield railroad depot.

Daily Intelligencer, Wheeling, Virginia, December 31, 1862, pg. 3.

THE GHOST HUNTERS.—Another large party was out on Monday night hunting the ghost, with the usual success.—The ghost is a more discreet ghost than we supposed. It don't care about being beaten with sticks or perforated with bullets. It will doubtless remain in its prison house until the excitement it has created shall subside.

It is the general impression about town…will be hurt before this…done with. A set of fellows…ghosting and garroting around is about played out. There is such a thing as too much of a good thing.

---

[83] *Outre* is French for unusual and startling.

1863

Daily Intelligencer, Wheeling, Virginia,
January 1, 1863, pg. 4.

THAT GHOST.—The ghost was seen again on Tuesday evening, and consented to indulge in a conversation with a gentleman who happened to meet him upon the commons. We think that the sooner this ghost is taught a lesson the better it will be for him and the particular locality in which he chooses to circulate.

Daily Intelligencer, Wheeling, Virginia,
January 7, 1863, pg. 3.

MORE GHOSTS.—Owning to the sensation created by the East Wheeling ghost other enterprising young men are engaging in the business. There is scarcely a section of the city now but can boast of its ghost. A very remarkable ghost has established his headquarters somewhere on Caldwell's Run, and has selected for his "beat" the plank walk between Hamilton's Foundry and Ritchietown. We very much fear that somebody will receive severe personal injury before this ghosting business is done with.

THE NEW YORK HERALD.

WHOLE NO. 9619.   NEW YORK, THURSDAY, JANUARY 15, 1863.   PRICE THREE CENTS.

The New York Herald, New York, New York,
January 15, 1863, pg. 3.

HEADQUARTERS.—ORDERS NO. 76.—THE WASH-ington
Market Social Club will meet at J. Johnston Esq.'s on Thursday
evening, Jan. 15, 1863, at 10 o'clock, to parade to the "Haunted
House," Twenty-seventh street, and there make a "charge" on the
"ghost" and capture said "ghost," and then bring the above to our
headquarters for exhibition. By order. Brigadier General, H.
CORNELL. Colonel, M.H. CHASE.

The New York Herald, New York, New York,
January 19, 1863, pg. 2.

City Intelligence.

THE HAUNTED HOUSE—A POPULAR HOAX—THE
POLICE "GUARDING THE GHOST."—For several days and
nights past the vicinity of a house in the fashionable neighborhood
of Twenty-seventh street, between Sixth and Seventh avenues, has
been in a perfect storm of supernatural commotion, owning to a
rumor having gained currency to the effect that a "spirit from the
vasty deep" or somewhere else had manifested itself in a corporeal
shape to the passers-by on sundry nocturnal occasions. So deep
was the interest manifested by the denizens of the locality in this
discovery that they congregated *en masse* for several successive
nights, for the purpose of witnessing the apparition of the grim
spectre whose unearthly debut in their midst became the source of
terror to some of a very fine nervous temperament, while the scorn
and ridicule of others of a stronger and more material caliber were
only aroused sufficiently to draw them to the scene for the object
of gratifying their curiosity, and have a hearty laugh over the
affair. The first real intimation which the ghost gave of his

112

penchant for sublunary society was on a dark night immediately before Christmas, when a party of ladies and gentlemen were enjoying themselves sociably with whiskey punch, wine, oysters, & c., in a large room of the house, formerly used as a bedroom, but which was subsequently transformed into a sitting room. Among the party were a lawyer, a clergyman and doctor—a trio which one might naturally suppose to be a match for any ghost, even though he came from the infernal regions themselves; were that transition possible. About half-past twelve o'clock, when fun and frolic were at their height, one of the young ladies was observed to grow suddenly pale. She then shrieked and dropped her wine glass, extending her hands horrifically towards the door. All looked in that direction, when a tall, gaunt looking representation of humanity, with a grim ashy aspect of countenance, and dressed as one in the humble walk of life, strode towards them, and finally composedly seated itself in an armchair, bending its lugubrious gaze the while on those assembled. Of course the natural sequence was a general skedaddle amongst the feminies, whiles a few of the males stood transfixed to the floor, not daring to ask it whether it was.

A spirit of air or goblin damned.

One of the party, screwing his courage as near the sticking point as possible, at length appreciated what was once supposed to have been the tenement of clay; but lo! it immediately vanished in thin air and again assumed mortal shape in a far off corner of the room. Terrified beyond measure at this, the whole party made a sudden exit from the room, the door of which was immediately banged to with terrific force, sending a hollow echo through the house. Every attempt to occupy the room either by sleeping or sitting up in it since has proved an entire failure, the parties undertaking anything so reckless having shown the greatest consternation on emerging from the haunted apartment. Shrieks, groans, sighs and wild hobgoblin exclamations have been frequently heard issuing from the infested chamber, and no pain of exorcism had up to last night been hit upon. The Police Commissioners consequently had a number of their men placed on duty about the house, to keep nightly vigil and see what was to be seen. Last night the Washington Market Social Club were to have gone to the house and taken out the ghost *volens*;[84] but they did not appear to be equal to the task, for up to the witching hour of night they did not make their appearance. From an early hour in the evening almost the whole strength of the police of the Twenty-ninth precinct were on guard in the vicinity of the haunted house, armed with dark lanterns, and looking as officious and uncommunicative as possible. As night advanced crowds of eager seekers after knowledge assembled, but their ingress to Twenty seventh street, both from Sixth and Seventh avenues, was strongly opposed by the batons of the dark lantern men. Suffice it to say at this late hour that the story of the ghost is all a hoax—that the vicinity of the haunted house (No. 88 Twenty-seventh street) is inhabited by women of easy virtue, who used their virtues to the casual corner, and that the police have been placed there to "guard the morality" of the city.

Dayton Daily Empire, Dayton, Ohio,
January 29, 1863, pg. 1.

Mysterious.—One night, not long since, an intelligent and benevolent lady called to see a sick neighbor, in the vicinity of the corner of Jefferson and Chestnut street. While near the corner

---

[84] Latin for "willingly"

indicated, when on her way home a spectral something suddenly appeared before her. It had the seeming of a woman dressed in black, and it made gestures of the most violent description. It remained but an instant and then disappeared with a sort of explosive noise!

Our informant is a lady of nearly fifty years of age, and is by no means nervous. She feels positive that the spectre— whatever it might have been—was not an optical illusion. She don't think it was the Chestnut street ghost, but a spook of the Satanic persuasion.

Muscatine Weekly Journal, Muscatine, Iowa, January 30, 1863, pg. 2.

They have a ghost in New York and a haunted house which attracts such crowds that the police have to remain in strong force to keep order. Both should be taxed as "amusement."

CUMBERLAND, MD., THURSDAY, FEB. 5, 1863.

Civilian & Telegraph, Cumberland, Maryland, February 5, 1863, pg. 2.

A GHOST ORDERED TO SKEDADDLE.—Some villain, assuming to be a ghost has been frightening the people of Newport, R.I., into fits, and the mayor notifies his ghostship that if he values his life he had better skedaddle to the shades on the double quick.

Daily Intelligencer, Wheeling, Virginia, February 11, 1863, pg. 3.

THE GHOST ON HIS TRAVELS.—Our ghost, finding some time since that matters were getting too warm here, disappeared and has recently journeyed to Newport, R.I. The Mayor there has issued an official proclamation against the ghost, solemnly warning it to cease its nightly walks or run the risk of being summarily sent to the shades below by a pistol-shot or police man's club.

Daily Intelligencer, Wheeling, Virginia, February 17, 1863, pg. 3.

THE GHOST.—We understand that a ghost has lately made its appearance in our neighboring village of Martinsville, and is in the habit of making nocturnal perambulations through the muddy streets of that place. It is thought to be the same ghost who lately distinguished himself in this city.

Alexandria Gazette, Alexandria, Virginia, March 23, 1863, pg. 2.

The Rochester [New York] Express states that on Monday evening last at the very unfashionable hour for ghosts, of between 8 and 9 o'clock, while a number of young men were sitting around the stove in Engine House No. 9, the trap door of the reservoir, of which the engine-house floor formed the top, and which cannot be raised by mortal hands without the assistance of a crowbar opened, and a ghost arose from the depths with a ghastly wound in its forehead.—The fireman vamoosed instantly in great consternation.

The Bellville Countryman, Belleville, Texas, April 11, 1864, pg. 2.

In London, recently a girl, aged nineteen, was so frightened by a friend who played the ghost on her, that she died in a few weeks. The fright caused the girl to bleed freely at the nose; she also lost her appetite and mind, and finally died of 'disease of the brain and hysteria.'

Daily Intelligencer, Wheeling, Virginia, May 16, 1863, pg. 1.

THE WHEELING BATTERY

WINCHESTER, May 12, 1863.

Editors Intelligencer:

As our kind friends in Wheeling are always anxious to hear from the Wheeling Battery, I thought it would be interesting to them, to read a rough description of our trip to New Market:[85]...

We went back as far as Mount Jackson where we camped for the night, quartering in the rebel hospitals—three in number.— In searching through one of the hospitals, one of the boys found two pieces of bones, they had been sawed off 1 ¼ inches square, and one piece was partly formed into a ring. They were shown to the surgeon, and he pronounced them pieces of the frontal bone of a human skull. I have often heard of the rebels making ornaments out of Yankee bones, but never could believe in such an atrocious thing. Now, from what I have seen with my own eyes, I am forced to believe it is but too true.

It commenced raining at 11 P.M. Our three guns were placed in position to command the banks on the opposite side of the river, as an attack was looked for from that direction; but the night passed without anything occurring of consequence, with the exception of some of our infantry being nearly frightened to death, by one of the boys swearing he saw the ghost of a departed bushwhacker,[86] in the hospital where they were quartered.

Rome Weekly Courier, Rome, Georgia, June 26, 1863, pg. 4.

A Northern journal contains a long rigmarole account of some spiritual exhibitions made in the presence of Lincoln and his

---

[85] Virginia

[86] Bushwhackers were Civil War slang for Confederate forces that practiced guerilla warfare on the borders between Union and Confederate territory.

Cabinet. Napoleon, Gen. Knox, and others, were consulted as the best mode of conducting the war. Lincoln must be in great strains when he has to look to the other world for military counsels. We should not think that Lincoln and his Cabinet need give spirits of the departed. A hundred thousand ghosts, whose blood is on his own hands, will visit him soon enough, either in this world or the next.[87]

Muscatine Weekly Journal, Muscatine, Iowa, July 24, 1863, pg. 2.

STONEWALL JACKSON.— The battle of Gettysburg[88] is the first great battle, and the Pennsylvania campaign[89] the first great campaign, which the main rebel army has undertaken since the war opened, without the presence and aid of Stonewall Jackson;[90] and the failure of their campaign has been so complete as their discomfiture in the battle. It may be that these facts had no connection with each other. But it must be remembered that each of Lee's five previous campaigns it *was Jackson who did the decisive thing— it was his action in each case which formed the turning point of the battle.* The rebels say that since his

T.J. "Stonewall" Jackson

---

[87] For more information about President Abraham Lincoln's involvement with Spiritualism during the Civil War see *"I Would Still Be Drowned in Tears": Spiritualism in Abraham Lincoln's White House* by Michelle L. Hamilton (La Mesa: Vanderblumen Publications, 2013).

[88] The Battle of Gettysburg, Pennsylvania was fought on July 1-3, 1863 and was a Union victory.

[89] The Pennsylvania campaign was from July 9, 1863 to July 23, 1863.

[90] Confederate Lt. General Thomas "Stonewall" Jackson (1824-1863) died from wounds received at the Battle of Chancellorsville. His death was a serious blow to Confederate morale.

death his ghost is still seen hovering near the scenes of battle,[91] if they are sure of this, the issue of the late campaign would seem to give color to the assertion of a spiritual medium who has lately been *en rapport*[92] with Jackson, and who averts that since his death he has turned Abolitionist and fights for the cause of the North.—*N.Y. Times.*

Battle of Gettysburg

Richmond Enquirer, Richmond, Virginia, August 7, 1863, pg. 1.

A GHOST STORY.—The inhabitants of a large long, tumbling-down old brick building, which has adorned Rocketts for at least a century, succeeded until Monday night in investing their abode with a mystery which excited the nerves of the immediate community to no slight extent, by saying, in short the house was haunted.—They evidently believed their own story, and as they were deemed honest folks, their sincerity was unquestioned.

---

[91] While there have been no reports of Stonewall Jacksons ghost haunting Civil War battlefields, the 2013 movie *Anchorman 2: The Legend Continues* featured actor John C. Reilly as the ghost of Stonewall Jackson.

[92] *En rapport* is French for "in harmony."

Spirits had rapped at their doors: white things had been seen to flit along the passages, and all that. On Monday night a "committee of investigation" from the neighborhood went into the house and waited for the ghosts. Presently a door was heard creaking, and then a couple of ghosts appeared on the steps: one of the watchers fired a pistol and the ghost vanished. The "committee," unable to account for this sudden disappearance, and finding no traces of their continued presence on the premises, concluded that they were "real ghosts," and adopted a ghost creed immediately. On yesterday morning, a seamen, named Julius Saul, called on his surgeon with a bullet hole in his shoulder, and told him a strange story about skylarking some old people, with a comrade, on the night before, down in Rocketts, and being mistaken for a ghost, "which he was a' playin," he got the wound. On being asked how often he had engaged in such fun, replied, "all his life." It was an amusement he could'nt resist, especially when the houses were of the right sort for making an impression.

Rome Tri-Weekly Courier, Rome, Georgia, September 29, 1863, pg. 1.

The Richmond correspondent of the Atlanta Intelligencer gives the following:

The following supernatural phenomenon is said to have occurred on the 1st inst., in Greenbrier County in this State, was communicated to the editor of the Richmond Whig by "an officer of rank, intelligence and character," and is vouched for by several eye witnesses, whose "veracity is unimpeachable." It will be likely to attract the attention of the votaries of the marvelous, and give rise to more or less speculation as to its occult significance. It may be proper to add to the account that the ghosts referred to presented quite a martial appearance, and seemed to be "marching north, or northwest, right through the mountains."

"The day was bright, clear and warm.—The locality a hill or mountain side, on which the sun was shining with full splendor. The first thing seen was something that the witness do not seem able to describe with clearness and accuracy. They say it was masses or bodies of vapor, mist or something else, five or six feet high, and two or three wide, floating in a perpendicular position, above the tree tops, moving on in a line with the utmost regularity and precision; then passing through the tree tops, without having broken the line or disturbed. These bodies are described as being of a whiteish green color, and passed off in white, marching in column, on the ground, through an open field, up the mountain slope, at a rapid pace, quicker than double quick time, the column separated only by a few feet. The witnesses state that they could see the men not only as a whole, but the individual parts—their heads, arms, legs and feet. Occasionally one would lag a little behind, and could distinctly seen to quicken his pace to regain his position in the line. They were passing for an hour or more, and, it is thought, numbered thousands on thousands. The field over which they passed is several hundred yards in length, and they covered the entire area in passing. Their general appearance was white, and they were without arms or knapsacks."

As the ghosts were seen moving in a Northwest direction, without arms or knapsacks, it has been suggested that their appearance prefigures a great peace convention, which is sooner or later to be called together in that section of country, for the purpose of making overtures for peace. The Editor of the Whig intimates that the phenomenon may have been a mirage; but a mirage occurs only when the earth is mantled over with a mist, and the objects presented are seen rising above the earth's surface, high up in the atmosphere. In the case before us, the day was clear and bright, and the ghosts were seen walking on the surface of the earth, through an open field, and up the slope of a mountain.

A somewhat singular phenomenon is said to have occurred a century ago or more, on the occasion of a great civil convulsion in France, when hostile armies were seen to encounter each other in the skies; but, on occasion, they were armed with weapons.—In this instance, they were without them, which evidently, it is said, means peace.

The New York Herald, New York, New York, October 9, 1863, pg. 2.

BEING A GHOST

James Lansing, of the Sixty-second Pennsylvania regiment, is a firm believer in ghosts. This belief is modern in its origin, and it originated thus: Last evening he and several members of his company were discussing the subject of execution for desertion, and reference very naturally was made to the recent execution for desertion, and reference very naturally was made to the recent execution in this corps. The body of the executed man is buried but a short distance from the company's camp. The conversation diverged into a discussion about ghosts, and wound up by one of the party betting a month's pay that Lansing did not dare go to the grave of the executed man and step over it three times. Lansing started, and the proof of his going there was to be three notches cut in the board at the head of the grave. The one making the bet equipped himself with a piece of canvass and a long stick, and hurrying to the grave, which he reached first, and lay in wait for the arrival of his betting companion. Lansing advanced close to the grave. The stick, the canvass and the soldier extemporized a ghost of seeming colossal height. A sepulchral grave came in as a fitting accompaniment.

"God have mercy on my soul. Save me, save me," ejaculated and ran Lansing.

"And you really believe you saw a ghost?" said one of the party, after Lansing had sufficiently recovered from his fright to tell the result of venture.

"I don't believe it—I know it," replied the victim of the joke. "He was twenty fenty foot high—and such groans!"

Is it to be wondered at that the aforesaid Lansing is a firm believer in ghosts?

THE INDIANA STATE SENTINEL.

VOL. XXIII, NO. 19.   INDIANAPOLIS, IND., MONDAY, OCT. 12, 1863.   WHOLE NO. 1,265

Indiana State Sentinel, Indianapolis, Idaho,
October 12, 1863, pg. 1.

A GHOST CLUB.—In London, they have established a
ghost club for research into the possibility of a traveler's returning
from bournes to which we all look forward with interest. The club
is in downright earnest, as may be gathered from the fact that the
committee advertise for a "haunted house," one whose reputation
is well authenticated.[93]

Daily National Republican, Washington, D.C.,
October 17, 1863, pg. 2.

A "ghost club" in England is in want of a haunted house, so
that they can cultivate the acquaintance of ghosts.

Dayton Daily Empire.

VOL. 1.   DAYTON, OHIO: THURSDAY, OCTOBER 22, 1863.   NO. 56

Dayton Daily Empire, Dayton, Ohio,
October 22, 1863, pg. 2.

If the ghosts of the hundreds of thousands whose lives have
been worse than thrown away, were to rise and haunt those who
are responsible for the grand mistake of a war, or for the unbroken
series of minor errors which have constituted the war policy and
prosecution, how sleepless would be the nights and how terrible

---

[93] The Ghost Club is the world's oldest association of psychical
research.

the days of the men who could not be satisfied without a little blood-letting.

The Cadiz Democratic Sentinel.

VOLUME 30, NO 25   CADIZ OHIO, WEDNESDAY, OCTOBER 28, 1863.   TERMS.—$1.50

The Cadiz Democratic Sentinel, Cadiz, Ohio, October 28, 1863, pg. 4.

Supernatural Signs and Omens
From the Richmond Examiner, October 6.

But, as if to vindicate the poets and super naturalists, the attention of the credulous has been called, of late, to two very extraordinary and apparently unaccounted occurrences. Mrs Temperance Carter, of the town of Marietta, Georgia, or elsewhere, being to all intents defunct, was made ready for burial, when suddenly she rose from the dead, and inquired the latest news from the war. The reply was, that Bragg was still retreating,[94] that the Court of Inquiry in the Vicksburg disaster had been dismissed,[95] and that Pemberton was to be restored to his command;[96] whereupon Mrs. Temperance Carter again, and without reluctance, died, permanently, it is supposed, since no tidings of her second resurrection have been received. No consoling interpretation could be given to Mrs. Temperance Carter's singular behavior, and still more marvelous, but less recondite,[97] event, was anxiously awaited

---

[94] Following the Tullahoma, Tennessee campaign in June 1863, Confederate General Braxton Bragg's (1817-1876) Army of the Tennessee retreated from the city.

[95] The surrender of Vicksburg, Mississippi to Union forces on July 4, 1863 was a critical loss for the Confederacy.

[96] Lt. General John C. Pemberton (1814-1881) surrendered the Confederate forces at Vicksburg, Mississippi. Pemberton was held as a prisoner until being exchanged on October 13, 1863.

[97] Recondite is the knowledge of obscure events.

by the aged females, of both sexes, throughout the country. Hence the great Greenbrier wonder, which is thus related:

During the afternoon of September 1, Mr. Moses Dwyer, an honest, responsible and unimpeachable farmer, Mrs. Percy, "who seems to have a very clear head," two other ladies, a youth almost grown, and a servant girl, all saw on the side of a hill or mountain ten miles west of Lewisburg, on which the sun was shining with full power, "something," which they were not able to describe with "clearness and accuracy," albeit Mrs. Percy's head was probably as clear than as it ever was. They declare, nevertheless that this "something" was masses or bodies of vapor, mist, or something else, of whitish green color, five or six feet high, and two or three feet wide, which floated above the tops in a perpendicular position, moving on in line, with the utmost regularity and precision, then passing through the tree tops, without having the line broken or disturbed, and then passing off in the distance. If this whitish green vapor, or mist, or something else, had done nothing more, the exhibition might have been regarded as a common freak of vapor on a mountain side, but "then came a countless multitude of men, dressed in white, marching up the mountain slope, at a rapid pace, quicker than double quick time;" the men seen "not only as a whole, but the individual parts—heads, arms, legs, and feet." Occasionally one would lag behind, and could be distinctly seen to quicken his pace to regain his position in the line. They were passing for an hour or more; numbered it is thought, thousands upon thousands; passed over a field several hundred yards in length, the entire area of which they covered in passing; "their general appearance was white, and they were without arms or knapsacks."

Newspaper clipping inset:

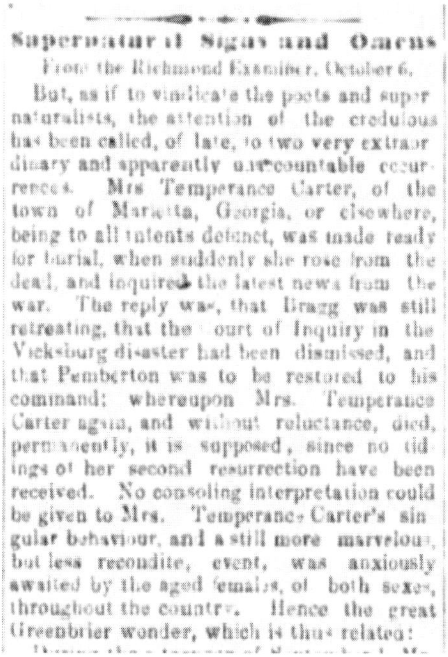

Supernatural Signs and Omens

From the Richmond Examiner, October 6.

But, as if to vindicate the poets and super naturalists, the attention of the credulous has been called, of late, to two very extraordinary and apparently unaccountable occurrences. Mrs Temperance Carter, of the town of Marietta, Georgia, or elsewhere, being to all intents defunct, was made ready for burial, when suddenly she rose from the dead, and inquired the latest news from the war. The reply was, that Bragg was still retreating, that the court of Inquiry in the Vicksburg disaster had been dismissed, and that Pemberton was to be restored to his command; whereupon Mrs. Temperance Carter again, and without reluctance, died, permanently, it is supposed, since no tidings of her second resurrection have been received. No consoling interpretation could be given to Mrs. Temperance Carter's singular behaviour, and a still more marvelous, but less recondite, event, was anxiously awaited by the aged females, of both sexes, throughout the country. Hence the great Greenbrier wonder, which is thus related:

This is the entire strange story, which, it must be confessed, beats Mrs. Temperance Carter, the dying prophets, the engraved eggs, and the intermitting springs, all hollow. The theory of the refraction of light, which accounts so happily for the wonderful phenomena of the mirage and the *Fata Morgana*,[98] might also explain the singular spectacle in Greenbrier, if the people of the Confederacy were not predisposed to superstition, and encourage therein by frequent calls of their attention to religious observances rather than the just appointment of them, and the right application which only human agencies are involved or need to be invoked.— Many pretended solutions by Southern visionaries, the latest of whom "hops" that the northward movement of the whitish green specters without arms, prognosticates the speedy return of the vandals, deprived of their means of destruction, to their own homes. It is fortunate for the propounder of this sage interpretation, that the vapory, or misty, or something else, bodies in Greenbrier were without weapons, for George Cruikshanks,[99] the comic artist of London, has just published a book to prove that since the days of Pliny the Younger,[100] nobody has pretended that armor, implements of warfare, shovels and tongs, or any formation of iron or brass, has a soul, and consequently that the ghosts of such things could not be.

As such might be declared of the readymade clothing furnished the Yankee army, which, far from having a spirit, has scarcely any body, if we may trust the newspaper diatribe against "shoddy" and "shoddy contractors." It will be prudent, therefore, to maintain, in spite of the veracious Mr. Moses Dwyer, the clear headed Mrs. Percy, and the "youth almost grown," that the greenish-white visions witnessed by them appertain more to their excited optics than to the realm of departed spirits, and that, as a general thing, it would be safer for the country to trust to good Generals, plenty of gunpowder, and strong armies, than to greenish white ghosts going up the side of the hill at Greenbrier. But the

---

[98] An unusual mirage that is appears in a narrow band above the horizon.

[99] George Cruikshank (1792-1878) was an English caricaturist and book illustrator best known for his illustrations of the works of Charles Dickens.

[100] Pliny the Younger (61AD-c. 113 AD) was a Roman author, philosopher, army and naval commander.

question, after all, rests with Mrs. Temperance Carter, who may emerge any day from the tomb, and be as anxious to impact information from the other world as she was some time ago to take it from this.

The Weekly Ottumwa Courier, Ottumwa, Iowa, October 29, 1863, pg. 2.

Very Strange if True!—Two Ghosts in Wapello County!—Great Consternation in Adams Township!

We learn, by a gentleman of unquestionable veracity, that great consternation prevails in Adams Township, in this county, occasioned by the nightly visitations of two seeming men, at the residence of Mr. Wm. Spaulding, who lives five miles east of Blakesburg. These visitors, be they who they may, and whether in the flesh or spirits in human shape, make their appearance about seven o'clock in the evening, and remain until about five in the morning, their first appearance being on Friday night, a week ago. They seem medium-sized, heavy set men *dressed in black*! On their first appearance, on Friday night, the family and some of the neighbors, were boiling molasses about forty rods from the house, when about seven o'clock, suddenly, clubs, cobs, (they had been shelling corn during the day) and small sticks, began to fly in a shower, from a certain direction, occasionally hitting some one of the persons present, but generally falling in one place. Once a candlestick, held by Mrs. Spaulding, was hit, nearly knocking it out of her hand. No person was then visible, but they heard something walking about with a heavy tread. About one o'clock, they quit boiling, and two of the men, Harmon Wellman and J.M. Spaulding, started out in the direction from whence the missiles seemed to come, armed with clubs and brick bats, to find and chastise the strange intruders. No sooner had the men started than the missiles was returned by the men, but without evidence of their hitting anybody. The party about the kettles returned about this time (one o'clock) to the house. After their return, the missiles seemed to strike the fence and the house with great violence. Spaulding and one of the men went out to turn out the horses, taking their guns with them. No sooner were they out of the house, than a large club fell near them, seemingly coming from behind. One of the men wheeled, and saw a man standing near enough to be distinguished in a dark night, at whom he

Very Strange if True!--Two Ghosts in Wapello County!-- Great Consternation in Ad ams Township!

We learn, by a gentleman of unquestionable veracity, that great consternation prevails in Ada ns township, in this county, occasioned by the nightly visitations of two seeming men, at the residence of Mr. Wm Spaulding, who lives five miles east of Blakesburg. These visitors, be they who they may, and whether in the flesh or spirits in human shape, make their appearance about seven o'clock in the evening, and remain until about five in the morning, their first appearance being on Friday night, a week ago. They seem medium-sized, heavy set men, *dressed in black!* On their first appearance, on Friday night, the family and some of the neighbors, were boiling molasses about forty rods from the house, when about seven o'clock, suddenly, clubs, cobs, (they had been shelling corn during the day) and small sticks, began to fly in a shower, from a certain direction, occasionally hitting some one of the persons present, but generally falling in one small place. Once a

instantly shot. The man ran and disappeared. They turned out the horses and returned to the house. Nothing more was seen of the men that night, although they were heard walking about near the house. The next night, and for the four succeeding nights, the same state of things existed, two being seen on Tuesday night. Missiles struck the fence and house, but left no dents and marks distinguishable by daylight. In the meantime, Mr. Spaulding and his neighbors became alarmed by such a strange phenomenon, and from time to time, met at Spaulding's house to try and solve the mystery. On Monday night, J.W. Wellman, Wm. Hayes, Wm. Spaulding and his son, spent the night watching. Sometime in the night, one of the men looked out of the window and distinctly saw, by the light of a bright moon, a man standing before the door. After sitting a while, they looked out again, and saw the man prostrate on a plank, lighting a dark lantern with a match. Getting their revolvers and guns ready, the party prepared to open the door, but strange to say, the four powerful men could not open it. They afterwards remained quietly in the house until about five o'clock in the morning. One night, Mr. E.B. Day took his dog, a very sagacious animal, and tried to set her on, but she trembled, ran between her master's legs, and refused to make any demonstration against the ghosts.

The above are the leading facts as related to us, of the most strange phenomenon. Mr. Spaulding at first attributed the persecution to political enmity, but certain evidence of the absence, in other places, of those he only could suspect, at times when the visitors were seen and engaged in their operations, satisfied him that he must look for some other solution of the mystery.

We give the facts precisely as they are related to us, merely expressing, by way of comment, our decided conviction that no Union men,[101] in or out of the flesh, have resorted to that mode of converting Mr. Spaulding and his political ways. The story is a strange one, and we await, with considerable anxiety, for the developments. In the meantime, an opportunity is afforded to the curious to speculate upon the subject of ghosts! We don't believe in ghosts, and if we did, it is against all ghostly rules to visit couples, and they have generally been clothed in white, invariably so as our recollection serves us. It is barely possible that some evil disposed persons have been playing rather a fatiguing and protracted trick upon Mr. Spaulding and his friends. Most of the phenomena can be accounted for without resort to the supernatural. To persons laboring under apprehension of danger, everything, particularly in the night, seems unnatural and distorted. Ghosts can be manufactured with the greatest ease. It is also extremely difficult to aim accurately under such circumstances, and a person would stand many chances of escaping to one of being hit. And so we might speculate upon all these occurrences, supporting them to be real occurrences. As to that we repeat, we merely give what is related to us.

---

[101] Union men were usually Republicans, and supported the Union war effort during the Civil War and the political policies of President Abraham Lincoln.

The Buchanan County Guardian, Independence, Iowa, November 17, 1863, pg. 2.

All Explained.

A good deal of talk has been had over some ghost developments in Wapello County, in this state, which took place at the house of a Mr. SPAULDING. The wonder was not lessened because the ghosts seemed to eschew the traditional ghostly color—white—and appeared in black habiliments. The acute Local of the Des Moines *Register*, however, saw through the affair at a glance. He knew that SPAULDING was a Copperhead,[102] and it did not take long for DIXON to conclude that these were friendly visitors from the kingdom of Pluto[103] to their friends here. DIXON argues the case at some length, and concludes:

Every Copperhead residence in Iowa will be honored with like visitations. The gentlemen in black are not content with a silent appreciation of the services rendered by their butternut brethren to the great cause of rebellion on this continent. A more palpable intimacy is about to be formed between rebels natural and rebels supernatural, to show to a skeptical world the identity existing between the Kingdom of Copperheads and the Empire of the Devil!

Charles City Republican Intelligencer, Charles City, Iowa, November 19, 1863, pg. 1.

As the horse car was passing the cemetery gate at West Troy, a few evenings since, a "ghost" came out of the cemetery and got upon the platform of the car. The conductor took to his heels without stopping to collect his fare of the terrible goblin. This, we believe, is the first instance on record of a ghost's patronizing a horse railroad.

---

[102] The Copperheads were a vocal faction of the Northern Democratic Party during the Civil War who opposed the war and demanded an immediate peace settlement with the Confederacy.

[103] Pluto was the Greek god of the Underworld.

Civil War Ghosts

Chicago Daily Tribune, Chicago, Illinois, December 3, 1863, pg. 3.

A Ghost on Board the Great Eastern.

The SS Great Eastern berthed in New York, 1860

On the 11, Capt. W. Paton, while addressing the members of the Mercantile Marine Association, in reference to the plan for repairing the big ship, mentioned a singular occurrence which took place in New York. An impression got abroad that the ship was haunted, the alleged ghost being no other than the impersonation of an unfortunate riveter, who was heard plying his avocation in one of the wells or compartments. Capt. Paton stated that before the vessel left this country he believed that one of the men employed in her construction was missing. The man was a riveter; he was missed from the ship, and never came for his wages; the supposition being that he had been riveted up in some part of the vessel. So firmly impressed were some of the men with this idea, that they left the ship in consequence. They affirmed that they had heard their departed friend busily engaged riveting in the middle of the night.

The story was believed by many persons in New York, and on one occasion while the ship was under repair, a diver signaled to be drawn up. He appeared pale with fright, and declared the ghost of the riveter was busy in the bottom part of the ship; in fact, that he began immediately over his head. Such was the consternation among the divers that they called in the aid of one of the spirit mediums, who are somewhat numerous in the city of New York. The medium came on board the ship, and after an examination declared that the missing man was there both "in body and spirit." Fortunately he (Capt. Paton) by pure accident was enabled to dispel the illusion. Being in a boat near the bows of the ship, he discovered that a swivel connected with the moorings worked to and fro, the movement causing a chink or vibration which at times, more especially at night, was heard throughout the vessel. It was this sound which had conjured up, in connection with the supposed fate of the unfortunate riveter, the phantom whose mysterious doings spread such consternation on board the big ship.—*Liverpool Times*, Nov. 14.

Belmont Chronicle, St. Clairsville, Ohio, December 10, 1863, pg. 2.

A GHOST, with woman's clothes, recently knocked at the house of old Mrs. Kennedy of Cleveland, Ohio, in the night. Her son John chased the ghost in his shirt and with an ax. A spirited run ensued, and the ghost ultimately bolted into Tom McClane's coffin shop, where he finally disappeared, probably into one of the coffins. Tom and John thereupon had a terrific battle of words, and next day the former brought an action for slander. The costs were $400; 80 witnesses were examined and the defendant gained the suit, the court charging that it would be difficult for a man to commit slander in his shirt in the street, on a cold night, and while chasing a ghost.

GOLD HILL DAILY NEWS.

VOL. 1.   GOLD HILL, N. T., WEDNESDAY EVENING, DECEMBER 16, 1863.   NO. 56.

Gold Hill Daily News, Gold Hill, Nevada Territory, December 16, 1863, pg. 1.

The Southern papers speak of an army of ghosts as having been seen in the air on the 1st of October. The rebels had better try to conscript that army to fight their battles. It could get along even with such clothes and rations as they provide.

Alexandria Gazette, Alexandria, Virginia, December 19, 1863, pg. 2.

On Wednesday night the bodies of six deceased Federal prisoners were deposited in the dead house of the hospital in Richmond to await the coming of the undertaker with coffins. Next morning one of the bodies was gone, and the plank knocked from the house, showed the way the ghost went. He had been "playing possum," and was laid out among the dead only to get up and run away when nobody was looking.

St. Cloud Democrat, St. Cloud, Minnesota, December 24, 1863, pg. 3.

SPIRITUAL.—The ghosts of innumerable dead turkeys have been flitting around for the past two or three days; while doubtless the few living ones that remain are thanking their stars that Christmas comes but one a year.

Michelle Hamilton

1864

Gold Hill Daily News, Gold Hill, Nevada Territory, January 13, 1864, pg. 2.

The Ghost of Rochester.

The City of Rochester, in the State of New York, is noted for its flour mills, water falls, and as being the place where spiritual knockings (by the Fox girls) was first invented.[104] It is now the center of a new sensation—and a spiritual one, too, at that. A private letter from that place, shown to us yesterday, tells about it. The story, in brief, is that an old resident of the city, a skinflint named Collins, lately deceased, suddenly, while on a visit to his former home in Connecticut; but instead of remaining quiet in his grave, like a respectful dead man, he has returned to his former haunts and frightens those who were his tenants by appearing to them at unseasonable times, and peremptorily demanding payment of his rents. The city, at last accounts, was greatly exercised by this bad conduct, and dozens of clear-headed and open-eyed people were ready to make affidavit that they had actually received visits from the ghost of "Old Collins."

---

[104] Margaret Fox (1833-1893) and Kate Fox (1837-1892) were the founders of Spiritualism in 1848. Some of the first Spiritualist séances were held in Rochester, New York.

We find the following in a late Rochester paper in reference to this strange affair. The imposition on that barber was really a cruel practical joke; but what did he want with the soap?—to wash his sins away?

THE EAST SIDE APPARITION.—The appearance of E.W. Collins on the East side of the River continues to be the subject of comment and conversation. That Collins died and was buried in Connecticut, there is no doubt whatever, yet there are, we understand, a number of citizens in that section of the city where he resided who insist that was here last week. It is said he is calling upon the different tenants in the block in which he was interested—no less than four of them having met him. On Saturday, as the story goes, he went into a barber shop and took a seat to be shaved. The barber put a napkin under his chin and lathered his face preparatory to removing his beard. Turning round to strop the razor, Collins disappeared, leaving the napkin but taking the soap. The spiritualists are in ecstasies and declare that they have no doubt whatever that the spirit of the dead man is roving about and sometimes appearing in his earthly habiliment.

Rutland Weekly Herald, Rutland, Vermont, January 21, 1864, pg. 2.

A MARVELOUS INCIDENT.—Walton's Journal (Montpelier) contains the following:—

A friend (whose name we do not give simply because we did not ask his authority for publication,) recently called on us, who has lost a son in the army, an officer of good promise, serving under Gen. Banks.[105] We alluded to the great loss of our friend, and in conversation upon that subject, he said a very remarkable

---

[105] Union Major General Nathaniel P. Banks (1816-1894) was the commander of the Army of the Gulf during the Civil War.

thing had happened to him in connection with it. When he had no reason to doubt the well-being of his son, and had no anxiety for him beyond what was usual, and was sleeping calmly, he was suddenly awakened by a shock as if he had been shot through the head.—His first thought was that he had been shot, or, to use his own expression—"this is death." But the next instant a vision of his son appeared to him, and the impression was that his son and not himself was killed. He had never believed in "ghosts," or spiritual manifestations; nor did he at the occurrence of this vision, nor does he now undertake to account for it, or call it a spiritual manifestation. He did not record the date or hour, but he did in the morning relate the circumstances to two of his friends. They did not record the date; but when, about three weeks afterwards, intelligence was received of the death of his son, by a shot through the head, at Port Hudson,[106] at six o'clock in the morning the recollection of one of them that the vision and the death were on the same day, and the other that the vision was on the same day, or the next day after the death of his son. Such was the account given to us, and we have no doubt of its truth. Our friend would not trifle on a matter which to him has not only the solemnity of the grave, but it also touches his keenest affections.

The Union, Georgetown, Delaware, February 12, 1864, pg. 3.

LETTER FROM BROADKILN

BROADKILN, Jan. 30, 1864.

DEAR UNION:

...It is said that the wicked ghost of old Blue-Beard and his fierce pirates haunt the white shore of the Delaware Bay, along the boundary of this place, and keep watch and ward over their manifold treasures, buried deep beneath sands.[107] And

---

[106] The Siege of Port Hudson lasted from May 22, 1863 to July 9, 1863, and was the final engagement in the Union campaign to recapture Mississippi.

[107] This is likely a reference to the English pirate Edward Teach (c. 1680-1718) known as Blackbeard.

"Proteus,[108] a name tremendous o'er the
main,
The delegate of Neptune's[109] watery reign,"

often leads his flocks to feed upon the green verdure along the
banks of the ebbing Broadklin. But this, as it is proper I should
say, happens mostly in the dark, small hours of night, when man,
nor creature of any kind, is roaming abroad. Therefore, dear
UNION, as it may seem to you, these things are more guessed at,
than really known. But for all that one would think it to be so, if
all were known....

ARISTARCHUS SCRIBLERUS

CEDAR FALLS GAZETTE.

VOL. 4.   CEDAR FALLS, IOWA, FRIDAY, FEBRUARY 19, 1864.   NO. 47.

Cedar Falls Gazette, Cedar Falls, Iowa,
February 19, 1864, pg. 1.

Correspondence of the Gazette.

LETTER FROM THE NAVY.

U.S FRIGATE MINNESOTA,
Hampton Roads, Va.

Are you aware that your regular old whale[110] is very
superstitious? believe in ghosts and hobgoblins? If you undertake
to argue the point you lose caste at once. Many are the yarns I
have heard them spin. One chap told me that he sailed in a ship on
board which a man had been killed the voyage before, and that at
every gale his ghost would appear; and whenever they went aloft

---

[108] In Greek mythology, Proteus is an early sea-god of rivers and
oceans.
[109] Neptune was the Roman god of freshwater and the sea.
[110] An "old whale" is 19th-century slang for an old sailor.

to reef topsails[111] the ghost would be there on the yard[112] at the weather caring. "Well," say I, "why didn't you let him haul out the caring?" The answer I got is: "Oh, you don't believe anything. It's no use to talk to you," etc.

Daily Ohio Statesman, Columbus, Ohio, February 21, 1864, pg. 3.

A GHOST IN CHICAGO.—They have a ghost in Chicago—a *black* ghost—that haunts the bridges and frightens belated travelers.—Many persons, who from their dealings with spirits and water ought to know all about such water spirits, have testified to the existence of the spectre, which has frequently prevented their reaching their homes "till daylight doth appear."[113] The *Journal* says that the spirit is supposed to be the ghost of a man who died of drinking Chicago water.[114]

Burlington Weekly Hawk-Eye, Burlington, Iowa, March 26, 1864, pg. 7.

One of the Chicago bridges is haunted by a ghost. Quite natural. They are the scene of a good many corporation murders.

---

[111] A topsail is a sail set above another sail on a ship.

[112] On a ship a yard is a spar on a mast where sails are set.

[113] The line "Till daylight doth appear" is a line from the English folksong "We Won't Go Home Till Morning" the author is unknown.

[114] Even in the 19th-century, Chicago, Illinois was already notorious for its polluted drinking water.

Dayton Daily Empire, Dayton, Ohio,
May 5, 1864, pg. 1.

A Solider Murder's Remorse.

During the battle of Olustee, Florida,[115] Jerome Dupoy[116] of Company D, Seventh Connecticut Volunteers, was shot in the back of the head and killed, evidently by some one in our ranks, and suspicion fell upon a substitute for a drafted man, named John Rowley, of the same company, who had had a quarrel with Dupay and been stabbed by him. Sergeant Broes charged Rowley with the crime, when he confessed it, and is reported to have made the following statement:

Battle of Olustee near present-day Lake City

"Well, Sergeant, I did kill Dupay; he stabbed me on St. Helena; I swore if ever I got a chance, I'd kill him; I had one at Olustee, and I killed him. Nor is he the only man I have killed or caused to die. I cut out the entrails of a sailor on a gunboat, since

---

[115] The Battle of Olustee, Florida was fought on February 20, 1864 and was a Confederate victory.

[116] Private Jerome Dupoy of Redding, Connecticut enlisted on November 6, 1863.

the war begun, and I killed by a stabbing, a man in New York, which caused me to leave my family and go a substitute for a drafted man[117] last fall. But the ghost of Dupay is the only one that ever troubled me. Since the battle, I have dreaded the nights, for they are horrible nights. When on picket, I always see Dupay stand a little way in front, his face all blood, and the bullet hole in his forehead. At night, when in my dreams he stands at the entrance, I awake, he is there pale and bloody but vanishes as soon as I see him. I could not keep this horrible crime a secret any longer."

He was of course arrested, and will be punished by death.[118] It is said that both the men were very bad ones.

Survivors of the Battle of Olustee in 1912 at a monument dedication.

---

[117] A person drafted into the Union army could pay for a substitute to take his place.

[118] Private John Rowley was executed for the murder of Jerome Dupoy on September 3, 1864 in Petersburg, Virginia. For more about the 7th Connecticut and the Battle of Olustee see http://battleofolustee.org/7th_ct_inf.html (accessed August 17, 2018).

Rutland Weekly Herald, Rutland, Vermont,
June 2, 1864, pg. 1.

A GHOST.—They have a ghost at the Mount Anthony Seminary,—a regular horrid, grim ghost—if we may credit the Bennington Banner's incredible story.

Burlington Free Press, Burlington, Vermont,
June 3, 1864, pg. 2.

The Bennington *Banner* has a story about the appearance of a ghost at Mt. Anthony Seminary—a trick of some fool or other.

Burlington Weekly Hawk-Eye, Burlington, Iowa,
August 20, 1864, pg. 7.

GHOST! GHOST!! GHOST!!!—An apparition, robed in white, was seen by a number of persons last night about eleven o'clock, gliding noiselessly along the top of the walls at the rear of the building occupied by Kellogg & Birge. Back and forth, back and forth, went the apparition, with noiseless, almost invisible step, several times and then disappeared. By those who saw it, and the moon being quite bright its every outline was distinctly visible, it is described as about six feet tall, and looking like a man attired in the habiliments of the tomb. It has been seen several nights in succession just as the clock struck eleven, and has excited considerable alarm in the immediate neighborhood.

GHOST! GHOST!! GHOST!!!—An apparition, robed in white, was seen by a number of persons last night about eleven o'clock,

About twenty-five persons witnessed its appearance last night and gazed speechless awe upon the picture. The interest is becoming most intense and large numbers will watch for it nightly until the mystery is explained.—*Keokuk Constitution*.

Sioux City Register, Sioux City, Iowa,
August 27, 1864, pg. 2.

The Keokukians are having a big excitement about a ghost that has made its appearance in the city several times of late.

Urbana Union, Urbana, Ohio,
August 31, 1864, pg. 3.

The grave diggers in a cemetery in Brooklyn, N.Y. are on a strike, and they threaten to make a ghost of him who undertakes to interfere.

Sunbury American, Sunbury, Pennsylvania,
September 24, 1864, pg. 3.

THIEVES.—Provision thieves have already commenced their depredations. Last week some vile miscreant stole from the cellar of the Rev. Mr. Gibson a basket of fine peaches that had been presented to him that day, together with a roll of butter and other articles. The ice house of Mrs. E. Greenough was also robbed a short time since. Some arrangements should be made to capture these midnight prowlers and send them where they properly belong the penitentiary. A few nights since one of these gentry was discovered in a new character, wrapped up in a sheet; he was performing the part of a ghost upon the premises of one of our citizens. This fellow ought to be in the army, but he is doubtless as worthless there as here.

Burlington Weekly-Hawk-Eye, Burlington, Iowa,
November 19, 1864, pg. 8.

ANOTHER GHOST.—A house occupied by a family named Simmons, out beyond the cemetery, it is asserted, is haunted by the ghost of a woman. The spectre it is pretended was seen Wednesday night, and the occupants of the building are badly frightened. The matter has created quite an excitement in the neighborhood.

Evening Star, Washington, D.C.,
December 6, 1864, pg. 2.

A RED HEADED GHOST.—For two weeks the vicinity of R and 7th streets has been greatly disturbed by a mysterious individual, whose nightly acts were so strange that the superstitious began to give out that a ghost was haunting the neighborhood. About the same time various persons reported with cut heads to Sergeant Johnson, of the second precinct, and some of them had been relieved of small sums of money. The sergeant suspected that the ghost knew all about the cut heads and robberies, and went to work to capture the shade. The men is uniform tried for several days to discover the mysterious visitor, but failed. The sergeant then detailed three of his men, ununiformed, and they succeeded in catching the ghostly visitor on Sunday night about 9 o'clock. He was taken before Justice Thompson, and was charged with disorderly conduct. The Justice fined him $6, which he paid promptly in mundane currency, and gave the unetherial name of John Smith. The police examined him closely, and discovered that his hair, naturally black, had been dyed red, and so nicely done that the fact could only be discovered by lifting the hair, when the original black was discovered growing out. He was held for the military detectives, who identified him as John Smith, alias Harry Myer, of the 2d Maryland regiment. He was delivered to the military.

1865

Alexandria Gazette, Alexandria, Virginia,
January 20, 1865, pg. 1.

An Irish family in Colchester, Conn., were very much disturbed the other day by seeing their husband and father enter the house, as they had a few days before paid $150 for the transportation home of his body from the army, and had buried him with many tears. It took some time for the live Irishman to convince his family that he was not a ghost.

Sioux City Register, Sioux City, Iowa,
February 11, 1865, pg. 2.

STATE NEWS.

The McGregor *News* has a rumor to the effect that an Irish girl in Clayton county is haunted by a ghost.

Daily Intelligencer

VOL. XIII.   WHEELING, W. VA. MONDAY MORNING, FEBRUARY 27, 1865.   NO. 33.

Daily Intelligencer, Wheeling, West Virginia, February 27, 1865, pg. 3.

A SOMNAMBULIST.—We have lately heard of the strange doings of a woman residing in the 3d Ward, who is a somnambulist, and who, unless the doors of the room in which she sleeps are well secured, leaves the house attired in her night clothes, and walks about the premises and through the streets. She was the occasion, something like a year ago, of much anxiety on the part of her friends, but she has recently appeared to have altogether abandoned the practice of taking nocturnal rambles, and it has not been thought necessary to place a watch upon her movements or secure the doors and windows. Latterly, however, she has resumed the practice. One night last week she left her house and repaired to that of a friend and acquaintance, and knocking upon the door, was admitted and placed upon a bed, where she remained until morning, and woke up very much surprised to find herself on strange premises. On another occasion she left her bed and took up her quarters in an old vehicle which stood in a carriage house adjoining the premises, where she was shortly afterwards found by her friends. On Friday night she left her room and took a promenade down the street upon which she resides, and encountered the belated individual to whom we are indebted for this information. Our friend's nerves being none of the strongest, he allowed himself to suppose that he had been sent for from the other world. He wheeled about, ran a distance of about two squares, concealed himself behind a tree box and commenced saying the only prayer he knew, "Now I lay me down to sleep." He was fortunately discovered in this demoralized condition by another gentleman, who inspired our friend with sufficient courage to induce him to approach the supposed ghost. The somnambulist was soon found, and being recognized, was escorted to her house.

Civil War Ghosts

Cleveland Morning Leader, Cleveland, Ohio, March 4, 1865, pg. 2.

Secesh Ghost Foreshadowed

When General Sherman's[119] army occupied Savannah the citizens pleaded starvation and asked to be fed. Amongst other applications, several ladies called upon the Provost Marshall of the Western District and unfolded a horrible story of suffering and woe. The gallant General —, impressed with the tale, seated himself to write the order of supplies. While so engaged, some remark was made about the termination of the war, whereupon one of the suffering supplicants opened upon the General

General William T. Sherman

as follows: "This war won't be terminated until you kill all the men, and then we women will fight you, and if you kill all of us it won't be ended then, for we'll come back as ghosts to haunt you." This sanguinary oration, delivered with all the venom of a Southern female beggar, quite appalled the General, who quietly tore up the order he was writing, saying—"if such be the case, I think you might as well die of starvation, as then your ghosts may be too weak to come back and haunt us." And he coolly, but politely, bowed the discomfited lady mendicant into the street.

Mineral Point Weekly Tribune, Mineral Point, Wisconsin, March 8, 1865, pg. 1.

Westfield, Conn., thinks it has a ghost. He, she, it, they or them walk up and down in a vacant house in the night season,

---

[119] Union Major General William Tecumseh Sherman's (1820-1891) forces captured Savannah, Georgia on December 21, 1864.

causing the most delightful terror to the people, who gather outside the house to listen to it.

The Bedford Gazette, Bedford, Pennsylvania, June 2, 1865, pg. 1.

Much excitement exists in Pittsburg about a house on Pennsylvania Avenue in that city, which is said to be haunted. Several columns of marvelous things are published in relation to it, enough to make any person believe that he saw a ghost himself every dark night, through the terror of reading of such dark horrors.

Delaware State Journal and Statesman, Wilmington, Delaware, June 6, 1865, pg. 2.

ROBBERY.—We are informed that a party of unruly soldiers entered the Freight house at Delaware City, one night last week, and stole a barrel of mackerel, and a box containing the reports of the Grand Lodge of Free and Accepted Masons of Delaware, for 1863-4. Unless they restore the reports they will be haunted by the ghost of Morgan[120] and all the Masonic hobgoblins that have been heard of for the last hundred years.

Rutland Weekly Herald, Rutland, Vermont, June 15, 1865, pg. 2.

Miscellaneous Items.

---

[120] William Morgan (1774-c.1826) was a New York whose disappearance and presumed murder sparked a wave of anti-Mason sentiment in the United States.

Civil War Ghosts

Ghosts are getting fashionable. Pittsburg has a haunted house; Cleveland has a haunted square; and now Detroit has developed a haunted building.

The Highland Weekly News, Hillsborough, Ohio, June 29, 1865, pg. 2.

Jeff. Davis[121] is reported to have had a real or pretended fit of insanity. Do the ghosts of the murdered at Libby, Belle Isle, Andersonville,[122] and the other prison pens of the South people his cell and keep his mind "troubled with thick coming fancies,"[123] or has he his co-conspirator Payne's[124] disease? He should be supplied with an aperient dose.

Jefferson Davis

---

[121] Jefferson Davis (1808-1889) was the President of the Confederate States of America from 1861 to 1865. At the conclusion of the Civil War, Davis was captured by Union forces and imprisoned at Fortress Monroe, Virginia until 1869.

[122] Libby, Belle Isle, and Andersonville were notorious Confederate prison camps. Union POWs housed at these prisons reported inhumane conditions and harsh treatment at the hands of their captors.

[123] "As she is troubled with thick coming fancies," is from William Shakespeare's *Macbeth*, Act 5, Scene 3, 40.

[124] Lewis Thornton Powell (1844-1865), alias Lewis Payne/Paine was John Wilkes Booth's co-conspirator in the assassination of President Abraham Lincoln. As part of the conspiracy, Powell attacked Secretary of State William H. Seward. While imprisoned, Powell tried to commit suicide by banging his head against his cell's iron wall. For his role in the assassination plot, Powell was executed on July 7, 1865. Many in the North in the summer of 1865 believed that Confederate President Jefferson Davis was part of the conspiracy to assassinate Lincoln. Legend holds that Jefferson Davis's ghost has been seen at Fortress Monroe.

Libby Prison, Richmond, Virginia, 1865

The Cleveland Leader, Cleveland, Ohio,
July 27, 1865, pg. 2.

Canards.

Since the war closed, the sensational press are exercising their ingenuity in the manufacture of canards, and in publishing plausible tales of horror, in whose verbose folds is wrapped a "gigantic sell." Years ago the monopoly of the business belonged to Cincinnati, which was not less celebrated for its swine than for its Munchausens.[125] Then, after an interval, came the "great Silver Lake Snake" story of a Buffalo journal, followed by the very clever farce of the "Twenty-seventh Street Ghost." The *Tribune's* sketch of the burning of the Museum, and what its reporter saw, took the cup for a brazen mendacity condoned only by the fact that it was so greedily swallowed by hundreds of papers through the country. Now we have a horrible story of the body of a Philadelphia merchant found in a barrel in a Richmond drug store, Mr. G. Whillekens being the discoverer, and Linn C. Doyle being the name of the contents of the barrel. What next will "turn up" remains to be seen; but meantime we suggest to those imitative Munchausens that they are engaged in very discreditable business. The first thing they know the Secretary of War will be after them with his "military necessity" dodge.

---

[125] Baron Munchausen is a fictional character in Rudolf Erich Raspe's 1785 novel *Baron Munchausen's Narrative of His Marvellous Travels and Campaigns in Russia.* In the novel, Munchausen narrates his impossible and fantastic achievements.

Gold Hill Daily News, Gold Hill Nevada Territory, July 31, 1865, pg. 2.

A GHOST.—A ghost has been seen on the road between Crown Point ravine and the Overman works, late at night within a week or so. It is a man ghost, and as his intentions not are appreciated by several men working in the Overman, perhaps the ghost had better "git up and dust." He may save his neck.

Chicago Tribune, Chicago, Illinois, August 24, 1865, pg. 3.

NOTES OF SUMMER TRAVEL.
The White Mountains....

[Correspondent of the Chicago Tribune.]
WHITE MOUNTAINS,[126] PROFILE HOUSE
August 16, 1865.

...There are some who rall against this Railroad, because they think it will destroy all the wilderness and romance of the ascent, and who hope that the ghosts of departed Indians that haunt the ravines and gorges, or the unspent curse of the old Sachem,[127] may hurl the first train, with its new-fangled engine, middle rails, cog-wheels and all, a thousand fathoms, sheer over the abyss. This seems to us, however, rather passionate and violent talk. We must not forget that this is the age of progress, and we shall hardly be able to restrain our applause when the Iron Horse makes the ascent, and looks off from the summit of Mount Washington. R.T.

---

[126] The White Mountains Range is located in New Hampshire.

[127] Legend holds that Mount Chocorua is cursed by Chief Chocoura who cursed white settlers after the death of his son. There are three different versions of the origins of Chief Chocoura's curse. For more information on the Curse of Chocoura see http://newenglandfolklore.blogspot.com/2014/01/the-curse-of-chocorua-and-its-history.html (accessed August 19, 2018).

Rutland Weekly Herald, Rutland, Vermont, September 7, 1865, pg. 2.

A good old-fashioned ghost is making a sensation in a fine mansion in Bristol, Pa., all to himself, just now, its flesh and blood occupants having deserted it. Chilly stories come from them about moans, shrieks, imprecations, soliloquies and sich, as if its ghostship feels uncomfortable about something, and light often glare out in the darkness or pass by the windows with such rapidity as to leave a long line of light behind. He isn't partial to the "moors pale beam" but performs in the day as well as the night time.

The Ottawa Free Trader, Ottawa, Illinois, September 9, 1865, pg. 1.

A Good Old Fashioned Ghost in Pennsylvania.

The town of Bristol, Pa., according to the Philadelphia *Press* correspondent, has a haunted house, where a ghost of the most approved style holds midnight revel to the great alarm of the townfolks. Here are some particulars:

WHAT THE GHOST DOES.

This fine mansion is deserted. On dark nights or at the midnight hour it is avoided, and the luckless wight[128] who has to pass it walks on tip-toe like the opposing pickets used to do on the Peninsula when a solider in the copse was unwittingly exposing himself to death. Moans have been heard to come through the gaping, broken windows—shrieks, imprecations, soliloquies—as if there was something or somebody in agony—something or somebody that wanted to die, yet was commanded to live—and

---

[128] A wight is a person considered to be unfortunate.

lights often glare out in darkness, or pass by the windows with such rapidity as to leave a long line of light behind. But the appearances are not by night alone, but by day also. The orgies of the ghost do not disappear, like mountain mists, before the sun. In sunlight as well as by the "glimpse of the moon," the spirit walks to the affright even of those who are bold enough to enter within the haunted precincts. Its manifestations differ in the daytime, however. A few days ago two skeptical young ladies, learning that the ghost could be seen at precisely six in the morning, determined to brave ghostly displeasure by entering his domain and plucking a wild flower or two. They went as promised, to the affright of servants, who were surprised at unwanted early rising—and now let them tell their own tale:

"The sun had got up when we got to the gate. When we opened it, it creaked on its rusty hinges, and went back again with a slam after we had passed through. That frightened us a little; but still we kept on right through the tangled hare grass in the path, and the twisted stems of boxwood, wet with dew, went around the side of the house right to the back, where there is a large flower-bed that has been growing to weeds, and growing and growing longer than I am growing old. We went right up to the flower bed, and Annie was just pulling a sprig of geranium, when there came a rapping—such a rapping—at a window just over our heads (a little shudder) and a shower of tiny pebbles—and where they came from we didn't know. We were frightened, I tell you. But we weren't going to give up. So we tried to get a flower again, and then there was a rapping again, only quicker and louder than before—a shuffling of feet, and a groan. We looked up at the window, but saw nothing, and then we ran away as fast as we could, and I fell down in the tangled path to the gate."

ANOTHER ACCOUNT.

The manifestation at night have more of horror for susceptible and superstitious minds and weak nerves, for darkness invests with terror what daylight shows even to be quite usual and commonplace. I will not enter into any detailed description of them, but give you the statement of an old farm-hand who, after speaking of the "haunted mansion," gave his own experiences.

"You see, sir," he said, while he stopped his horse (he was plowing at the time,) and gathered up the rein-ends in a lump in his brawny fist—"you see, sir, I was just the way I am now (he wore a shirt and muddy kersey[129] pants tucked into his boots, and a battered straw hat;) I was going down to the store for the old man, and I had a bit of a kettle in my hand and a big basket slung over my shoulder; I walked along first rate till I got down to *that* place" (nodding his head towards the mansion with a motion half muscular, half nervous). "I felt queerish like, and hitched myself up to go by right and square. It was only about nine o'clock, or thereabouts—may be it might be close to ten—but what should I see when I got to the far end of the fence but a tall person in white, with a brown kind of a handkerchief on its head—and it had a candle in one of them old-fashioned candlesticks. It walked along on the tops of the flowers and box-bush like, and didn't bend them."

"Ah!" was my involuntary exclamation, while I assumed an air of great interest and entire belief.

"Yes, sir," said the ploughman decisively, "and it walked right towards me, and then, I got up and left, and that's all I know."

"And do you really believe in the existence of the ghost?"

"Well, I guess I do!" answered he, decisively. "Has not everybody believed in it these twenty years gone?"

We did not demur, but left him, and wondered how anybody in Bucks county could believe in ghosts at this day. It was an evidence of want of knowledge, as well as of superstition. But Bristol was an old borough; it was a Democratic county; that explained the matter—partially.[130]

---

[129] Kersey is a coarse woolen cloth used in the 19th-century for work garments.

[130] In the Civil War era, the Democratic Party was viewed as the party of traditional values. Hence in this article the locals of this county believed in ghosts because they were Democrats.

WHO THE GHOST IS.

That I cannot begin to tell you. There are many intimations of black deeds in that old house years ago, and fifteen other conjectures are one usually indulged in in such cases. Those who have seen the ghost, all differ in their descriptions of him or her, so that the "oldest inhabitant" cannot fix anybody, once in the flesh, but now departed, who looked like it. The property is said to be owned by a lady in your city, who does not occupy it because she is afraid. She knows not who the ghost is, only that he or she is.

Commercial Bulletin, Richmond, Virginia, September 12, 1865, pg. 4.

Toronto[131] has a ghost, which walks in Colborne street every night, to the great discomfort of the citizens. The people think it is a burglar and the newspapers with such sensation head lines as "Another Visit of the Spectre!" "The Ghost Still at Large!" sell rapidly.

Chicago Tribune, Chicago, Illinois, September 24, 1865, pg. 2.

A HAUNTED CHURCH.

Those who are superstitiously inclined have a fine opportunity to exercise their imaginations over the new sensation in Jersey City. It is reported that a church in that classic Metropolis is haunted by ghosts or other supernatural occupants. Strange sights are seen, and strange noises are heard, for which there is thus far no explanation. Last Sunday evening a mob collected for the purpose of demolishing the church in question, but the impossibility of ascertaining what church was haunted, and the interference of the police, put an end to the proceeding.

---

[131] Canada

Norfolk Post, Norfolk, Virginia,
September 27, 1865, pg. 1.

A delicate young lady on High street discovered a *rough one*, tall, tragic, and poetic, looking in her chamber at a late hour in the night. Her screams put the "villain" to flight. He was no doubt a *guerilla*, or a ghost, and it is fortunate that he didn't devour the damsel, or spirit her away. Perhaps it was a dream. Young ladies, are much given to dreaming, that they are haunted by good looking villains.

Rutland Weekly Herald, Rutland, Vermont,
September 28, 1865, pg. 8.

The Jersey City Ghost

For several days past stories of mysterious performances, consisting mainly of howlings at night in one of the churches of Jersey City, have been in circulation, and the Jersey City newspaper (the *Times*) has printed the stories of what it called the ghost. The subject has attracted the attention of the Jersey City Common Council, and at the meeting of that body Tuesday night Alderman Gaffney offered the following facetious preamble and resolutions:

Whereas, It appears by a statement in the New York *Herald* of the 17th instant that one of the church edifices in our city is infested with spirits, spooks, ghosts, hobgoblins, and sundry and divers other unnatural apparitions, from which spectral non-existences is, sue certain melodies, unearthly, subterrestrial and diabolical noises, sounds—thunderings and murmurings, by reason of which the chief of Police and some of the policemen of our city were affrighted, stunned and unceremoniously ejected from said church edifice, at the wee small hours of the morning, when the pall of night has overshadowed the Western hemisphere; all of which statement is corroborated by our worthy Chief; therefore be it.

St. Boniface Church (building with child).

Resolved. That such unseemly, unbecoming and misbehaved mythical visitors, within the limits of our city, tending as they do to alarm old women, children, and the members of the Police Department, should at once be summarily dismissed, banished, and caused to skedaddle; and to that end, that the premises hereinbefore recited be referred to the Committee on Police with instructions to investigate the cause of such terror striking manifestations; and should said committee find such statement to be true, it shall be their duty to visit such church edifice at the hour in which "such apparitions most do congregate"—that is to say at the hour of 2 o'clock, a.m. of some day between this day and next regular meeting of the board; and on arriving at the threshold of said edifice, shall gird up their loins and boldly and valiantly enter the same, proceed midway into said building, and with stentorian voice bid the base intruders "down," as Macbeth "the ghost of Banquo" did, and should they find that the said diabolical noises, thunderings and murmurings are produced by any of the Colchesters,[132] Davenports,[133] or other

---

[132] Charles J. Colchester was a popular Spiritualist medium who was exposed as a fraud. For more information on Colchester, see *"I Would Still Be*

spiritual or spirituous mediums, now so prolific in this neighborhood, the said committee shall at once report the facts to the United States District Attorney, with the request that indictments may be at once preferred, and perpetrators of so fool and unnatural outrage be brought to justice for practicing that art without a license.

Resolved, That said committee report the result of their visit to the diabolical preternatural excrescences at the earliest practical opportunity.

Delaware State Journal and Statesman, Wilmington, Delaware, October 3, 1865, pg. 2.

The awful ghost in a Jersey City Church turns out to be a dog that had found his way into the building, unknown by the sexton. He was starving to death, and of course made a fuss about it.

The Western Democrat, Charlotte, North Carolina, October 3, 1865, pg. 1.

A BIG GHOST STORY
Remarkable Affair in a Church

Considerable excitement has arisen in Jersey City in consequence on groans, yells, and unearthly sounds said to emanate from a church in the upper part of Jersey City for some

---

Drowned in Tears": Spiritualism in Abraham Lincoln's White House by Michelle L. Hamilton.

[133] Ira Erastus Davenport (1839-1911) and William Henry Davenport (1841-1877) were Spiritualist mediums whose act was exposed as a fraud in 1865.

nights past. The first known of these mysterious sounds was some ten days since, when the pastor had occasion to return to the church after evening service to procure some manuscript which he had forgotten and had occasion to make use of. The edifice had been closed for the night, and was in total darkness.

The New York Times says:

"On entering, he lit a match to guide him along the isle; and when approaching the altar at the rear, his attention was attracted by a low moaning sound, which gradually increased and at the same time drew nearer to him. To this he at first paid but little heed, presuming it to be the antics of mischievous boys; but presently the sounds changed to seemingly unearthly yells, shrieks and groans, from innumerable invisible beings clustering around in close proximity to his person, until finally his feelings were so wrought upon that he felt impelled to leave the building with all possible haste.

"The above are substantially the facts of the case stated by the pastor of the church to Chief of Police McMannus after reports were beginning to be circulated in the neighborhood that the church was haunted, and requesting that the matter might be kept as quiet as possible, believing that in a few days at furthest he would be able to unravel the mystery and satisfactorily explain the cause of the sounds. Since that time the church edifice has been thoroughly examined, inside and out, but without unraveling the mystery; and meantime these

CAPT. ANDREW J. Mc MANUS

dismal and unearthly yells and cries are heard almost every night. A couple of nights since, Chief of Police McMannus, accompanied by Aid Doyle and Detective EL McWilliams, determined to pay a visit to the reported haunted church.—They accordingly procured the keys and entered the edifice shortly after midnight.

"Taking their position in the centre of the church in total darkness, they had remained there but a short time when they heard a low moaning sound, apparently proceeding from the vicinity of the pulpit, which gradually grew louder and came nearer until it finally culminated around their heads into howls, yells, groans, & c, and then gradually died away as it came. After a few moments of perfect silence, Chief McManus drew from his pocket a revolver, loaded with blank cartridges, and fired one charge, when almost instantly the edifice seemed filled with thousands of infuriated demons, making the most hideous noise and apparently bent on tearing them to pieces. The officers describe having experienced a very peculiar sensation in the head, and finally the noise became so hideous and unearthly that they made a hasty retreat, apparently pursued by the infuriated demons to the door, which they closed and locked. The officers then crossed the street to the opposite walk, and remained there until daylight, but heard no further sounds, and made no discoveries which would tend to explain the mystery. The people residing in the immediate neighborhood claim to have been disturbed at all hours of the night by these demonic sounds, and a number of them have determined to leave the neighborhood."

[Our readers may believe as much of the above as they please. We don't believe in ghosts.]

East Saginaw Courier, East Saginaw, Michigan, October 4, 1865, pg. 2.

SENSATIONS.

...Of purely domestic sensations "the ghost" is the latest elimination of the specials; not a ghost after the manner of the stage representations lately in vogue, a creation of photographic legerdemain,[134] but a genuine, *bona fide* old fashioned visitor from the lower regions, who makes his or her appearance amid groans and moans, and shrieks, with suggestive odor of brimstone and a

---

[134] Legerdemain is the skillful use of the hands when performing conjuring tricks.

sepulchral bluish flame that burns with a miscellaneous disregard for the tastes "feelinks" of spectators....

Wheeling Daily Intelligencer, Wheeling, West Virginia, October 4, 1865, pg. 4.

"SPOOK."—Some graceless scamp in East Wheeling is engaged in devoting his nights recently to playing ghost, much to the annoyance of old ladies and young children in that vicinity. We advise him to quit it at once, as we know of at least one person who is "laying for him," at whose hands he will receive just chastisement if he is so unfortunate as to be captured. He may waken up some morning and find a short notice of his untimely death in the *Intelligencer.*

The Savannah Daily Herald, Savannah, Georgia, October 6, 1865, pg. 1.

Letter from New York
[From our Regular Correspondent.]

New York, Saturday, Sept. 30, 1865.

Ghosts

Over in Jersey City there has been a sensation kicked up by an alleged haunted church, which, after puzzling the mysteriously inclined people of that burgh for a while, with its weird like noises and ghostly moans was at last proves to be haunted by nothing more alarming than the watchdog of a resident of the neighborhood. Almost a similar case has occurred in 14th street in this city. This was not a church but a private house, of neat and respectable appearance which was accused of containing the ghost, if not the skeleton, of a murdered man, the victim of a tragedy for excelling in the horror the famous Bordell murder. On investigation, it proved there was no ghost, had been no murder, and that the marks of "blood," found on the doorstep, consisted principally of lager beer, doubtless an emanation from the stomach of some drunken fellow, who, in the unsteady condition of his nether limbs, had sought the shelter of the front stoop of the house in question.—"Ghosts" are at a discount in this vicinity.

Gold Hill Daily News, Gold Hill, Nevada Territory, October 12, 1865, pg. 2.

THE ghost of Mrs. Surrat[135] is said to be the only recognized leader of the Copperhead party, and she doesn't clearly define her position.

The Union Flag, Jonesborough, Tennessee, October 13, 1865, pg. 2.

THE JERSEY CITY GHOST.

Tremendous Excitement—Churches Mobbed—Pale Bluish Lights Seen—Cold Corpse-like Bodies Felt—Horrible Noise Heard—An Explanation.
[From the New York Daily News, 20th.]

The matter has created an *emeute*[136] in Jersey City, which is perfectly tremendous. On Sunday night hundreds of men and women, excited to the highest point of morbid curiosity and

---

[135] Mary Surratt (c.1820-1865) was executed on July 7, 1865 for her role in the Lincoln assassination. Legend holds that Surratt's ghost has been seen at the Surratt House in Clinton, Maryland and at the site of her imprisonment at the Washington Arsenal now known as Fort Lesley J. McNair.

[136] *Emeute* is French for riot.

superstition, congregated in the vicinity of all the uptown houses of worship in the city. About forty persons went over from Hoboken also—among them a committee of examination—and a numerous crowd from New York, attested the sensation which the report had up to that time created.

A mob of three or four hundred persons assembled in Erie street, and were finally dispersed by the police; another of the German Catholics in South English street, until a late hour in the night.

Last night there was no abatement of the excitement. The ghost has, however, been very generally located somewhere near the St. Boniface, although nothing is as yet known to the populace, and our reporter was pressingly requested to make no mention of any particular locality. Among the various, explanations thus far suggested by the knowing ones, is the idea that some fellow found ingress under the flooring of the St. Boniface, and is amusing himself by practicing upon the credulity and superstitions of the people, betaking himself there at night and regaling the alarmed victims with dismal yelps and howls.

THE JERSEY CITY GHOST.

Tremendous Excitement—Churches Mobbed—Pale Bluish Lights Seen—Cold Corpse-like Bodies Felt—Horrible Noises Heard—An Explanation,

[From the New York Daily News, 20th.]

The matter has created an *emeute* in Jersey City, which is perfectly tremendous. On Sunday night hundreds of men and women, excited to the highest point of morbid curiosity and superstition, congregated in the vicinity of all the up-town houses of worship in the city. About forty persons went over from Hoboken also—among them a committee of examination—and a numerous crowd from New York, attested the sensation which the report had up to that time created.

A mob of three or four hundred persons assembled in Erie street, and were finally dispersed by the police; another of the German Catholics in South Eighth street, until a late hour in the night.

One gentleman, well known in the city, insisted that the ghost is located in the vicinity of Father Seneg's in South Eighth street. He relates that while his daughter was out on Sunday night, hunting for the ghost, she saw in passing the above named edifice, a spook or ghost upon the steeple, which waved its hands mysteriously toward the spire, hurled a pave-stone directly down in front of her face (fortunately not hitting her) and suddenly disappeared.

She describes the spectrum as having been gigantic in appearance, with eyes hollow and fiery, like marsh lights, and wearing a long flowing robe which resembled a cloud, so vapory and mistlike was its apparent texture. At the same time she heard noises of the most unearthly order, which seemed to issue from within the building.

Night before last, during the progress of the storm, singular lights were seen to move to and fro slowly and warily in the edifice of St. Boniface. A policeman, who was present, and first noticed it describes the color as having been yellow with a bluish tinge, and totally unlike anything he had ever before seen. They would be seen only for an instant flitting to and fro and then die out, succeeded by shrieks and hollow moanings.

Thus far the matter progressed among the populace, and all day yesterday the wildest wonderment prevailed, and the ghost was the sole topic of conversation. Men talked of spectres and shadows upon the street; women gossiped half shivering with terror, about the strange mystery, and *juvenes* absolutely shuddered—even to the imperturbable newsboy—at the weird revelations which went from lip to lip.

But last evening the excitement waxed wilder and more tumultuous; several German societies turned out with arms in their hands to drive away his ghostship, a procedure sufficient to drive away any ghost of respectability, and in general Jersey City was in perfect state of insanity.

Some facts of a very peculiar order came to light last evening, that only served, when disseminated, to heighten the fever of the public.—Several gentlemen of undoubted veracity and respectability were invited to visit one of the previous named edifices in company with the sexton. As they entered the gate and passed around the building the same singular lights previously mentioned were observed by one of the party. Decided to press on, he however, made no mention of the matter, until one of his companions hazarded the remark.

"Why, the building is lighted!"

And sure enough the building was lighted; a saintly bluish flame appearing exactly in the position of the candelabrum.

"The gas has evidently been lighted to frighten away the ghost," rejoined one of the party rather skeptically.

The investigators entered. The edifice was silent as a tomb within, and the tall columns gleamed like *spectre* under the pallied illusion of the light. No sound save that of the muffled footsteps of the party disturbed the repose of the dimly illuminated atmosphere. It was a *mise en scene*[137] to excite, indeed, unto dreams of the supernatural grander than those of Afrasiao, and more superstitious than ever froze the heart of Moslem Saracen or haunted the reveries of opium intoxicated Turk. The faint flame of the candelabrum only served to make the darkness more gloomy aisles of the church more terribly suggestive.

"Let us turn off the gas," stammered one of the party, shudderingly.

The gas was accordingly turned off, but strange—ah! the strangest of all!—the dim, uncertain flame still flickered above the candelabrum, continuing to burn without the slightest disturbance from a gust of air which at that moment stirred uneasily the drapery of the pulpit and the arms and fabric of the candelabrum.

"What the devil is the matter with the thing?" gasped the skeptical gentleman rather profanely, by way of keeping his courage up. "I'll put it out; see if I won't."

While striving to put out the light by waving hats near it his hand came accidently in contact with it. It was cold—stone cold—cold as the hand of a corpse, and the skeptic shrunk back with a shudder, as the fire of the candelabrum went out in darkness.

But as the light went out a low, moaning, ominous sound arose from the flooring of the building, gradually expanding in volume until ghostly shrieks and groans (distinctly articulate) broke in on every side, reverberated with unearthly laughter in every part of the building, and died away in hollow murmurs, like the falling of dirt upon a multitude of coffins.

This was three times repeated, and again a bluish flame appeared above the candelabrum.

These facts are attested upon the veracity of every one of the several gentlemen present.

Upon the promulgation of the above, the crowd became next to unmanageable, and seemed determined to force the doors of the St. Boniface and one or two other edifices in the vicinity.

---

[137] *Mise en scene* is the arrangement of scenery on the stage for a theatrical performance.

Not a few, however, treated the whole matter as a hoax, and insisted that the whole story was a fabrication of some over-fervid, or over-excited imagination.

Our reporter was assured yesterday at the police headquarters (Jersey City,) that there was more in the matter than the stoutest hearts dare acknowledge; but we must wait for further developments. He was, moreover, assured that a card would be published in the course of a day or two by the clergyman and trustees of a certain prominent house of worship in the city, giving all they know about the matter.

The State Rights Democrat, Albany, Oregon, October 14, 1865, pg. 1.

HAUNTED HOUSE.—Within a stone's throw of Stewart's new marble house on Fifth avenue is a dwelling really believed to be haunted. It is an imposing and elegant building. It has been occupied and abandoned by the three families within a few months. It is now in the market. We talk of the nineteenth century; how enlightened it is, and how bravely we have got over the superstitions of the other ages. While the fact is there is just as much belief in witches, hobgoblins, ghosts, spirits and haunted dwellings as there ever was. Spiritualism is only as outlet of the same element. Many men accounted shrewd and intelligent buy and sell and transact their business only by consulting some clairvoyant. One man made $40,000 in a whiskey speculation. Guided by a medium he made a further investment, lost his $40,000 and $20,000 added to it. Yet he has undimmed confidence in mediums. No body can tell what is the matter with this house on Fifth avenue. Externally it seems all right. The character of the men who have moved out—who have bought it and sold it—indicates plainly that there is trouble some where. The popular faith is that it is haunted.

Alexandria Gazette, Alexandria, Virginia, November 1, 1865, pg. 3.

Last night was all Hallow's Eve, or Hallowe'en—the vigil of All Saints. In the old country this was, and still is, a time observed by the young people, for "trying their fortunes." The Washington Chronicle says—"Burns has immortalized this festival by his famous poem of Hallowe'en."[138] The leading idea respecting Hallowe'en is that it is time, of all others, when supernatural influences prevail. It is a night set apart for a universal walking abroad of spirits, both of the visible and invisible world. Those born on that day are believed to have the faculty of seeing all kinds of beings of the other world, such as ghosts, spirits, goblins, & c., and they are also supposed to be born to extraordinary good luck. The old custom of "playing tricks" is not forgotten here. One of them, the throwing of cabbage stalks at people's doors, was carried out, in this place, lost night, and the boys had quite a night of it.

Evansville Daily Journal, Evansville, Indiana, November 9, 1865, pg. 4.

A GHOST.—They have had a ghost excitement down in Morgan County, an old, decrepit, and rheumatic dog playing the ghost.

---

[138] Scottish poet Robert Burns' (1759-1796) poem "Halloween" was first published in 1786.

VOL. IX.   ASHLAND, ASHLAND COUNTY, OHIO, WEDNESDAY MORNING, NOVEMBER 15, 1884.   NO. 45.

The Ashland Union, Ashland County, Ohio,
November 15, 1865, pg. 1.

A Haunted Jail.

The inmates of the Newport jail firmly believe that the building in which they are confirmed is haunted. They say that every night about the witching hour of twelve, "when the churchyard yawn," & c., a very ghostly looking man, wearing a plug hat, glide into their cells, although they are locked, and, after looking around a moment departs. One of the prisoners, who has been greatly troubled by these nocturnal visits, that he attacked his ghostship a few nights since, and, after a desperate struggle succeeded in ejecting him from his cell through the have which is used for the purpose of passing food to the prisoners. All evil doers will consult their interests by giving Newport a wide berth, for if arrested they will surely have to sleep in the haunted jail.— *Cincinnati Gazette*.

Charles City Intelligencer, Charles City, Iowa,
November 16, 1865, pg. 2.

A man in Linn County had his skull cut open, and his life seriously endangered, as the result of trying to play the ghost to scare folks. So says the Cedar Rapid *Times*.

Houston Tri-Weekly Telegraph, Houston, Texas, December 13, 1865, pg. 6.

PERSONAL

Wirz's[139] ghost is a regular attendant at the spiritual sessions in New York State.

---

[139] Confederate Captain Henry Wirz (1823-1865), was the commandant of the notorious Confederate prisoner of war camp Andersonville. Wirz was executed on November 10, 1865 in Washington, D. C.

Michelle Hamilton

About The Author

Michelle L. Hamilton earned her master's degree in history from San Diego State University in 2013. In her free time, Michelle is a Civil War and 18th-century living historian. Born and raised in California, Michelle now resides in Ruther Glen, Virginia. Michelle is the author of *"I Would Still Be Drowned in Tears": Spiritualism in Abraham Lincoln's White House.*

You can follow her at her blog:
http://michelle-hamilton.blogspot.com.

Michelle Hamilton

Other titles from Haunted Road Media in which Michelle Hamilton has appeared:

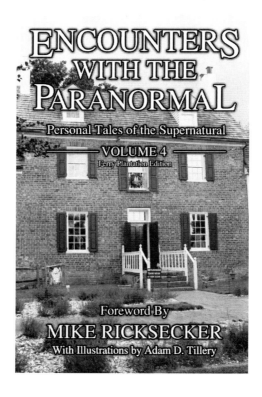

Almost everyone has a ghost story. Real people. Real stories.

Read about haunted houses and vehicles, experiences during paranormal investigations, visits from relatives that have passed on, pets reacting to the paranormal, psychic experiences, and conversations with full-bodied apparitions.

ENCOUNTERS WITH THE PARANORMAL reveals personal stories of the supernatural, exploring the realm beyond the veil through the eyes of a colorful cast of contributors.

Michelle Hamilton

For more information visit:
www.hauntedroadmedia.com